THE
PEACEKEEPERS

MICHAEL DYE

www.christianlawenforcment.com

www.thepeacekeepers.org

Published by: Advantage Books™

www.advantagebooks.com

Library of Congress Control Number: 2005928478

First Printing: May 2005

08 09 10 11 12 01 02   9 8 7 6 5 4 3 2

Printed in the United States of America

ACKLOWEDGEMENTS

There are a number of people who assisted in the development of this study without whose support this book could never have been produced. Foremost, I want to give thanks to Jesus Christ, our Lord and Savior, whose divine intervention played a paramount role in the formation of this study. Since I have never considered myself a writer or had the desire to write, there were times that I reviewed this book and was amazed at the words that God placed on my heart to share with you.

I want to thank my Pastor, Mike Cobb of Valencia Hills Community Church, who led me back to a life with Christ by showing me that worshiping God isn't just about ceremony and that anyone can have the ability to lead others to Christ without the need for a degree in Theology.

I would also like to acknowledge Pastor Rick Warren of Saddleback Community Church, whose books, *"The Purpose Driven Life"*, and the *"40 Days of Purpose"* were the inspiration for the creation of this small group study.

Many thanks to Bonnie Hanson, author of a number of Christian children books. It was pure divine intervention that I found Bonnie. I thank God for her knowledge and wisdom and appreciate her volunteering her time to help me edit this book.

I would like to extend my gratitude to the original PeaceKeepers members who encouraged and inspired me to fulfill one of my purposes for the Lord. This book is because of you Francis Boateng, Gary Hallden, Leon Lancaster, Cliff Lloyd, Kym Lyznick, Jeff Siroonian and James Young.

There are many other family members and friends who inspired, advised, and encouraged me along the way: Pastor, friend, and co-worker Ramsey Tuaua.

Pastor Jim Zeilenga; Terri Cobb; Charlie Helms; Tony Marino; Chuck Fauci; my parents, Bob and Dorothy Dye; and my brother, Chris Dye.

Special thanks to my God-given spouse Jennifer and our daughter, Emily, who put up with all the long hours that I spent away from them writing.

I would especially like to thank you the reader for taking a leap of faith to purchase and read this book. I pray that you will discover how God has uniquely shaped you for a life of service and purpose. May your life be richly blessed as you work through this study.

TABLE OF CONTENTS

INTRODUCTION

There is no other occupation like that of a law enforcement officer. Trying to control the peace, enforce the laws, and maintain the safety and security of the community that both you and your family belong to is no small task. There are drunk drivers, violent spouses, child abusers, rapists, murderers, thieves, and terrorists anywhere that you go in the world and the only line of self-defense between you and these "crooks" is that "thin-blue line" which is universally referred to as the Police.

Christian officers have an unprecedented opportunity to make a difference for Christ through their daily contacts with both the public and their fellow officers. There is a common bond among officers world-wide that is instantly recognizable among all those in the profession of law enforcement. However, if you read what the Bible says in Romans 13 about the role of the police officer and governmental authority; you will begin to see the need for an even closer bond among officers, a biblical bond. Once we recognize that we have a greater purpose in the world and that we are working together in a profession that God has ordained, then the bond of comradery now becomes a spiritual one with every police officer in the world obligated to follow God's command.

The PeaceKeepers study is dedicated to uniting law enforcement officers around the world to be passionate followers of Jesus Christ by helping them understand God's purpose for their lives and career. As you progress through this study you will begin to see a recurring theme that revolves around four main topics; *stress, money, family*, and *discovering your Godly purpose*. Exploring these topics is essential for the spiritual growth and well-being of any officer. All police officers struggle daily with these topics because they are all inter-related. Simply stated, the more you work, the more money you make and spend. And, the more you work the less time you have with your family and giving back to God. By not letting God control your life, a vicious cycle of family, financial and work stress will occur. All of these factors can begin to weigh heavily on the individual officer causing them to lose sight of the true Godly purpose behind their lives and careers. But, what if you understood that you had an alternative? That each day you went to work you carried out a God given purpose and responsibility not to your job, but rather through your job, as you learn to serve others through your police duties. At this point, the focus on the material benefits of the job and that of any personal issues will begin to pale in comparison as you see the greater need to reach the spiritually lost around you. You would then view your job becoming your mission field for helping others to live a life with Jesus Christ.

Because of the negativity and evil that surrounds all those in the profession of law enforcement; many officers have lost sight of the Godly meaning behind their careers. However, by learning to have an attitude of *"service"* and not *"serve us"* and leading others to learn about the Good News of Jesus Christ through our positive and Christ-like encounters with the public, some amazing turnabouts in both your personal and professional life will take place. For example, just think for a moment at what our communities would be like if only fifty percent of the police officers in the United States began to carry out their job responsibilities with Godly purpose? I can only imagine the amount of crime that would be reduced, the decline of line of duty deaths, and the numbers of spiritually lost that may be saved. I believe Churches would be filled, crime rates would fall, and jail populations would dramatically decrease.

It is my sincere prayer that this study helps you to learn to live your life with Godly purpose as you reach out to serve both your communities and your fellow law enforcement officers as one of God's PeaceKeepers.

HOW TO USE THIS STUDY GUIDE

You are about to embark on a life-changing experience as part of a PeaceKeepers small group. Studying God's word together always impacts and strengthens our spiritual lives in powerful ways. Your participation in this study will be the most essential part to developing and fostering your understanding of God's purpose behind your career in law enforcement.

While you may decide to read this study as an individual, it is important to understand that the Bible tells us that we were formed for fellowship. Romans 12:5 (NIV) states *"In Christ we who are many form one body, and each member belongs to all the others."* This means that you can't fellowship by yourself. It takes at least two people to have fellowship. Jesus was the originator of the small group concept. He traveled around with a small group of twelve disciples teaching in people's homes and along the roadside.

In many ways your study group is not unlike your law enforcement job. In police work we generally work as a team, forming partnerships in order to accomplish the goals of enforcing the law and protecting one another. You should use this same "team" concept in forming and building your small group. Make the effort to find a co-worker or a group of officers to work together with you on this study. By doing so, I believe that your life and the lives of others in your group will be spiritually enriched.

WHO CAN JOIN?

The PeaceKeepers study is open to all those in the field of law enforcement, security, and corrections, as well as their immediate family members. It does not matter if the officer is current, former, part-time, or retired. All officers should be involved in the study, regardless of the agency that they work for or their Christian affiliation. The study group should accept all interested persons whether they are experienced Christians, first time "seekers", or even non-believers. The Peacekeeper's study is open to all officers regardless of race, sex, or creed.

LEADING A GROUP

While the study chapters have some flexibility to them, each lesson is designed to be taught once a week. There should be a host leader that schedules all of the meetings, promotes the study, and leads each class. You can utilize a variety of venues for your small group meetings to include your place of worship, your home, a public park or a quiet room at your place of employment. I would highly recommend that the host leader lead the first week or two and then offer the opportunity to lead future group meetings to other members on a volunteer basis. Allowing others to lead instills confidence and encourages active participation. No one should ever feel forced to lead a study. Below is a timeline that you can use to help keep your meeting on track. Feel free to shorten or lengthen the time based on group needs but I would not recommend a meeting shorter than 45 minutes or longer than 2 hours.

- **5 minutes** - Meet & Greet (pick-up refreshments if available)

- **3 minutes** - Open in a brief prayer - Pray for the meeting and bless the officers that attended, as well as those that were not able to attend. Always remember to pray for safety for the officers that are working.

- **45-60 minutes** - Start session - take turns reading the Bible passages and stories. Remember to strive for group participation.

- **5 minutes** – Take prayer concerns. Close in prayer.

If you or other group members have more than one Bible at home, consider bringing them to the meeting to share with others who may not yet own one. Encourage members to read from different translations of the Bible as you work through the study. I have found it very educational and insightful to hear different translations of the same passage.

SHARING AND GROUP DISCUSSION

Sharing your faith with others can be scary to a new Christian and in the beginning may seem awkward. But this is normal and these feelings are both common and understandable. There are several discussion questions built into each chapter of the study and are purposely put there to help foster discussion amongst group members. Remember that there are no right or wrong answers. Participation and discussion is the key to the group's success. Have the faith and courage to step out and speak up. God not only wants to see you spiritually flourish in this group but He may also use you or your words to reach someone else. We all have special stories and circumstances to share, both about our jobs and our walk with Christ. Please be respectful to other group members by keeping group discussions and prayer requests confidential.

SMALL GROUP MOST WANTED

Once you have established your PeaceKeepers small group, use the *"Most Wanted"* chart located on the next page to keep track of your group members. Feel free to make copies. Try to make a point to contact with one or more of your fellow group *"partners"* by e-mail or telephone at least once during the week in order to help provide spiritual accountability.

ON A PERSONAL NOTE...

This book is written from my own individual spiritual point of view with the "seeker" or "first-time" Christian peace officer in mind. Therefore, the book is purposely written in easy and overly simplified terms. While individual officers may read this on their own, the study is meant to be presented in a "team" setting with other law enforcement officers where everyone may feel more at ease.

I realize that there are various Christian denominations whose ideology may differ slightly than what is expressed in this study guide. However, this should not hinder your group study in the least. I would encourage each chaplain, church official or small group leader to use the material found in this study as a "tool". Feel free to incorporate your own Christian-based faith ideas into the study lessons. For example, if a particular denomination believes strictly in the use of the King James Version (KJV), then please feel free to use the KJV in places where I may have used the New International Version (NIV). The goal, no matter what the delivery, is the same; to see officers come to know and accept Jesus Christ into their lives and acknowledge Him as their Lord and Savior.

It is my sincere prayer that your participation in this small group Bible study will be a blessing to all those within your group. May God bless and keep you safe as you perform the job as one of His "PeaceKeepers".

Your Small Group Most Wanted

In Christ we are many form one body, and each member belongs to all others. Rom 12:5 NIV

Name	Phone Number	Email

Michael Dye

Chapter One

Can A Cop Be A Christian?

"Just the Facts"

Bible Verse: *"Defend the cause of the weak and fatherless; maintain the rights of the poor and oppressed. Rescue the weak and needy; deliver them from the hand of the wicked"* – Psalm 82:3-4 (NIV)

Can a cop be a Christian? This can be a tough question for many law enforcement officers to answer. Usually, this is because most officers have a hard time merging both their faith and their job together. In fact, most cops go about treating the two as if they were mutually exclusive of one another for fear of offending others or ostracizing themselves from their co-workers or supervisors. This misconception about separation of job and faith can cause many law enforcement officers to discard their Christian beliefs while at work, serving to make the officer feel as if they are not functioning in a position in which God would want them. As we will learn throughout the PeaceKeepers study, this idea could not be further from the truth. As a group read Psalm 82:3-4 aloud. This verse should be seen as a direct command calling us to a life of service to help others persevere in a life surrounded by stress and evil. God has uniquely designed us for a life of service by blessing us with specific skills and abilities. We will discuss this in more detail

---

Small Group Scripture Reading - Read the following Bible verse as found in 1 Corinthians 12:4-11. Discuss among your small group members what spiritual gifts you feel that you may possess.

---

later in the study. However, no matter how well God has hardwired us to serve in the field of law enforcement, a cop cannot be a Christian until they have accepted Jesus Christ into their heart. What we do or how we act are important, but acts alone do not make us Christians. In 1 Samuel 16:7 the Bible states, *"The LORD does not look at the things man looks at. Man looks at the outward appearance, but the LORD looks at the heart. "(NIV)* And James 2:14 says, *"Dear brothers and sisters, what's the use of saying you have faith if you don't prove it by your actions? That kind of faith can't save anyone. "* (NLT) If you have never accepted Christ into your life there are three basic steps to follow:

- First, admit that you are a sinner and in need of God.

- Second, believe that Jesus Christ died for your sins and rose again.

- Third, confess Jesus Christ as Lord of your life.

Do not be discouraged if you do not feel that you are currently ready to accept Christ into your heart. Please continue to be a part of this study and allow God's word to work in your life. Every day brings a new opportunity to accept Christ as your Lord and Savior.

Working for God?

Law enforcement officers are in a unique profession in that we see the best and worst of society. Every day we police an evil and spiritually lost community. We see child abuse and broken families. We deal with violent crimes, such as rape and murder, and we have the opportunity to glimpse into the evil eyes of the people who commit these crimes. On occasion, we are even called to use deadly force. For these many reasons, an officer may not feel very "Christ-like" while on duty and may ask themselves if this is really the profession in which God wants them.

It is important to remember that God created the position of a peace officer knowing full well the evil hearts and sinful intentions of man. Our Lord has known since creation that citizens would require help at certain times in their lives and that the public order would need to be maintained. You may ask, "If God really loves us and gives us all our skills and abilities why would he want us to use them in a job where we deal with evil on a daily basis?" Perhaps this question could best be answered if we were to view our jobs not just as a source of income but as a way of serving God. Romans 13:1 states *"Everyone must submit himself to the governing authorities, for there is no authority except that which God has established. The authorities that exist have been established by God."* (NIV)

This may come as a shock to some officers because most of us had never considered our profession as God-given. But the laws that we enforce and the authority that we possess were all handed to us from God. The same laws that so many of us take for granted are actually based upon the same laws that God handed down to Moses in the form of the Ten Commandments. These commandments are found in Exodus 20. Let's briefly take a look at them and see if any of them sound similar to the laws that you enforce every day.

1. You shall have no other Gods before me.
2. You shall not make for yourself any idol or graven image.
3. Do not take the name of Lord your God in vain.
4. Remember the Sabbath day and keep it holy.
5. Honor your mother and father.
6. You shall not murder.
7. You shall not commit adultery.
8. You shall not steal.
9. You shall not lie or give false testimony.
10. You shall not covet your neighbor's possessions.

Most of us do not envision ourselves enforcing biblical laws during the course of our daily routine. But that is exactly what we are doing. The authority that you possess as a law enforcement officer was directly handed to you by God through the governmental agency for which you work. Simply translated, you are not just a city, state or federal employee; but rather you are working as a servant of God the Father. What an awesome responsibility that is! In other words, this means that we are working not just for a pension but for a purpose, a Godly purpose.

As we progress through this study you will begin to see how focusing on your God-given purpose will help to merge your career and your Christian life.

> ***Small Group Scripture Reading*** – Take turns reading as a group the following Bible verse; Romans 13:1-13. Afterwards, discuss among the group members the following questions.

- *What specific Bible verse means most to you and why?*

- *How do you think that this Bible verse is relevant to your job as a law enforcement officer?*

- *After reading the Ten Commandments, what similarities do you see to the laws that we enforcement daily?*

A Cop Used By God

I believe it is safe to assume that few of us in the profession of law enforcement ever take the time to realize or accept that God has a purpose for the individual officer. You see, God can use you in order to fulfill some special assignment that only He knows where and when it will take place. It may be to help someone that needs physical life saving. It may be to help bring closure to a grieving crime victim. It may be to make an arrest and remove someone from society. You could be the answer to someone's prayers and your actions may strengthen someone's faith. On an almost daily basis you will be confronted by tragic situations or circumstances. God can use you in these situations to make a spiritual difference by placing you at just the right moment in someone else's life.

Let's be honest for a minute. All of us have thought about being used by some greater power while in our jobs. But, how many of us have stopped to think or realize that this greater power may actually be God working through us? How many times have you disregarded being "in just the right place at just the right time" for someone. Far too many of us have dismissed these events as simple coincidences.

Now, before you think that God only uses law enforcement officers for his purposes; you should know that God can, and will, use anyone that has accepted Him into their lives. 1 Corinthians 12:6 states, *"There are different ways God works in our lives, but it is the same God who does the work through all of us."* *(NLT)* What the Bible tells us is that it doesn't matter if you are a Wall Street financial wizard, a firefighter, a nurse, a retired police officer, a paramedic, a correctional officer, a store clerk, a probation officer, a construction worker, a school teacher, a church leader, a volunteer, a homeless person, or even a convict. God can and will use any occupation and any set of circumstances that we find ourselves in as a way to serve a specific plan for Him and His Kingdom.

As Christian cops who have accepted Christ into our lives and who practice the teachings of Jesus Christ, we should always remember that we have a Godly purpose to advance His kingdom by leading others to a life with Christ. However too many of us as officers feel that leading others to Christ is not our responsibility. Too many of us think that our job is to simply enforce the law and lock up society's bad guys. But as we will discover throughout this study, our responsibilities are much greater than that.

Small Group Discussion Questions – Answer the following questions as a group.

1. What situation(s) have you found yourself in where you felt as though God was using you to help someone in need?

2. How do you think God is working through you now? What purpose do you think you are fulfilling?

Small Group Scripture Reading - Read the following Bible verse as found Romans 8:28 KJV *"And we know that all things work together for good to them that love God, to them who are called according to his purpose."*

God Is Our Back-Up

At times we may feel that God is not with us. There will be periods in our life where we will encounter problems and stress; at work, in our finances and in our home life. Perhaps, you may even feel that your spiritual life is out of balance. It is normal to question where God is during these difficult times. We also question how a loving God would allow the suffering and stress that we see first-hand in our jobs. James 1:2-4 teaches us that we are to be happy when our way is rough because it is at these times that God is shaping our character. Romans 5:3 tells us, *"We can rejoice, too, when we run into problems and trials, for we know that they are good for us--they help us learn to endure"* (NLT)

Be comforted in knowing that you are not alone. God is always on-duty right by our side. He is the best Commanding Officer that you could ever have. Turn to Him in times of need and He will be there for you, providing comfort and peace. Even if you have not been faithful in attending church, reading your Bible or praying; God is still there waiting for us to return to him. God states in Hebrews 13:5, *"never will I leave you; never will I forsake you."*(NIV)

A Christ-Like Foundation

Throughout this chapter we have touched on the fact that we are blessed by God with special skills and abilities to carry out our jobs in law enforcement. And, we have learned that our career helps to serve God's purpose for our lives. But how do we face the day to day stress of our job with Christ-like conviction? Every day that we put on the uniform of a law enforcement officer and head out to *"protect and serve"*, each of us should strive to maintain a Christ-centered, spirit-filled life while on the job. Philippians 2:5 states, *"Your attitude should be the same as that of Christ Jesus."* (NIV)

Start your day in prayer. Pray before you start your shift, that God will protect you and your fellow officers and that he will use you to make a positive difference in the life of another person. If you know other fellow Christian officers on your shift, consider a group prayer at the beginning and ending of your shift. The Bible instructs us in Philippians 4:6-7 *"Don't worry about anything; instead, pray about everything. Tell God what you need, and thank him for all he has done. If you do this, you will experience God's peace, which is far more wonderful than the human mind can understand. His peace will guard your hearts and minds as you live in Christ Jesus."*

Stay connected with a church family. Sometimes working shift work does not allow us to attend church regularly on Sundays. However, it is important to maintain the bonds of Christian friendship. Ephesians 2:19 states, *"You are members of God's very own family, citizens of God's country, and you belong in God's household with every other Christian."* (LIV) If you happen to be working on a particular Sunday set aside another day during the week where you can take time to read and reflect on God's word and praise and worship him for what he is doing in your life. In doing so, I believe that you will find both peace and fulfillment that God desires for each of us.

Small Group Discussion Questions – Answer the following questions as a group.

- ***True or False-*** *An officer with a foundation built on a personal relationship with Jesus Christ is better equipped to deal with the stress encountered while on the job?*

- ***Question -*** *Why do you think that an officer who has a strong Christ-centered foundation is better equipped to deal with the stressors of the job? Write and discuss your examples below and discuss with the group.*

Being Devoted to one Another

Legendary country and western singer, Hank Williams, Sr., lived a destructive lifestyle that ultimately led to his death in 1953. He wrote a song near the end of his career that should become an anthem for the Christian law officer. The song was entitled "Men with Broken Hearts." The lyrics state the following; *"If you haven't stood in that man's shoes, or seen things through his eyes, or stood and watched with helpless hands while the heart inside you dies. So help your brother along the way, no matter where he starts, for the same God that made you, made him too, these men with broken hearts."* I realize that to a bunch of tough police officers these lyrics may sound a little soft. You may even think that I am trying to turn you into some *"peace-loving"* cops. But be assured, these musical lyrics actually represent what Jesus commands us to do. Romans 12:10 states, *"Be devoted to one another in brotherly love. Honor one another above yourselves".(NIV)*

How soon we forget that we are all created by the same God; no matter the race, sex or creed. Under our flesh we all look alike. You cannot tell one person from the next. During my years spent working as a Detective, I was required to attend a number of autopsies at the Coroner's Office. For those of you who have attended an autopsy who will understand what I am talking about when I say that "beauty is only skin deep." Just as God is able to look past our outer skin to the beauty within us, we should also try to do the same. Being devoted to each other means we should always try to find the good in someone. Review 1Samuel 16:7.

Small Group Scripture Reading – Genesis 1:27; "*So God created man in his own image, in the image of God created him; male and female.*"

In summary, I feel it is important to answer our initial question; "Can a Cop be a Christian?" The facts clearly show that a cop can not afford NOT to be a Christian! This profession is ordained by God and shown to be necessary in the Bible. Prudent law enforcement officers should have a strong Christian foundation by establishing a personal relationship with Jesus Christ. God clearly has a purpose for your life and you should be armed with the knowledge of God's word. So, that if you are called upon to help someone in need you will have the teachings of Jesus backing you up. With everything that you can face as an officer, you need the protection, peace, and guidance that only God can provide. Put your trust in Him today.

Chapter Two

Redirecting Your Life

Bible Verse: *Those who live according to the sinful nature have their minds set on what that nature desires; but those who live in accordance with the Spirit have their minds set on what the Spirit desires."* – Romans 8:5 *(NIV)*

Without an understanding of God's grace and mercy and without accepting Christ into your life you will never be able to fulfill the purpose that God has planned for you. By now you are probably asking several questions such as, *"I haven't been in Church in years, how does God even know who I am?"* Or you may be thinking to yourself, *"I know God can't use me, because I am the biggest sinner of anyone I know!"* Let me let you in on a little secret; we are all sinners. The Bible states, *"For all have sinned, and come short of the glory of God"* – Romans 3:23 *(NIV)*.

But here is one of the most important aspects behind the story of God's grace and mercy. If you call on God and ask for His forgiveness it will be done. No matter what your sin may be. God will work in the lives of anyone that is willing to accept Jesus Christ into their heart. It doesn't matter your background. He doesn't care what sins you may have committed in the past. Be repentant and let God take control of your life. Too many people get stuck in the present because they can't get over their past. They won't allow God

Small Group Scripture Reading – Select someone from your group to read the following Bible verse; 1 John 1:9 *"If we confess our sins, he is faithful and just to forgive us of our sins, and to cleanse us from all unrighteousness."*

to use them because they don't want to believe that God would want to use them.

The Bible likens us to a vine with God being the gardener. John 15:2 (NIV) states, *"He cuts off every branch in me that bears no fruit, while every branch that does bear fruit he prunes."* There are many areas in our lives that could use some pruning by God; our poor attitudes at work, our macho "cop" image, and our misuse of authority.

Our Attitudes

In Chapter One we discussed some of the destructive influences that can change an officer's Christian attitude. Policing an evil and spiritually lost society will naturally cause you stress. While training, physical fitness, and proper officer safety procedures are all important aspects of an officer's professional career; it is having a spirit-filled positive attitude established through our Christian connections that will keep an individual officer on top of his or her job. There will always be times when trying to maintain a Christ-like attitude will be difficult. Being yelled at by protesters, drunks, gang members or people with hateful attitudes directed towards the police would hardly put anyone in a good mood. During my own law enforcement career I have encountered many situations in which it would have been easy to develop a bad attitude toward the public I was serving. While assigned to special detail duty during college Spring Break events I have been called foul names and have had beer thrown on me…at least I believed it was beer. More recently, while working a security detail for the federal government during the Democratic National Convention in Los Angeles, I was spit upon during an anti-war demonstration by a crowd of individuals wearing black masks. So, I have been on the receiving of stressful and hateful attitudes towards law enforcement.

But, by knowing that there is a Godly purpose not only to your life but to your job, you should be able to re-direct your bad attitude to a more positive way of thinking. Allow your personal relationship with Jesus Christ to work through you and reach those who are spiritually lost instead of letting negative thoughts creep in about how the protestors, gang bangers, and juvenile delinquents are ruining your day; instead thank God for giving you the opportunity to share the good news of God's love with them. In 1 Peter 3:15-16 the Bible states, *"Always be prepared to give an answer to everyone who asks you to give the reason for the hope that you have. But do this with gentleness and respect, keeping a clear conscience, so that those who speak maliciously against your good behavior in Christ may be ashamed of their slander."*(NIV)

Remaining connected with other Christians and other Christian cops can help you maintain a positive attitude. Attending your PeaceKeepers small group study on a regular basis provides an opportunity for others to support you in your walk with Christ. Galatians 6:2 says this, *"Share each other's troubles and problems, and in this way obey the law of Christ."* (NLT) I would suggest that you pray daily and set time aside each day to read the Bible. With a strong Christian foundation in place, you will begin to see God working in you to change your negative attitude to a positive attitude of serving others.

Small Group Reading – Read James 1:12-13 (NIV); *"Blessed is the man who preservers under trial, because when he has stood the test, he will receive the crown of life that God has promised to those who love him."*

Our Macho Image

Ask the general citizenry about law enforcement officers and most of them will refer to the macho bravado that they usually emanate. What they don't know is that this macho image is usually a front, a defense mechanism, put in place by the officer to wall him off from all the inhumanity that he faces on a daily basis. The reality is that cops see things in one day that could make the average citizen attend years of therapy. However, as officers we are expected to get back in our black and white and head right back out on patrol again; remaining neutral to the tragic experiences that we have just encountered. Instead we suppress our anger and our hurt, as we silently cry to ourselves, "Why, Oh, why?" We have confused the idea of neutrally enforcing the law with how we are supposed to deal with grief, stress, and spiritual matters.

Remember that you are not required to remain neutral in the area of helping others. Don't forget the oath you took to serve and protect. The fact of the matter is that it is okay to show your emotions as well as help those that may be spiritually hurting. I once heard a saying about the many roles of a police officer. It went something like this: A policeman is a preacher, a teacher, a protector, a peacekeeper, a judge, a jury, a mentor, a counselor, a friend, a parent, a child. A policeman is all the things that we hope and pray for. Most of all never forget that you are only human, and a creation of God Himself.

Jesus and the Force Continuum Scale

As a peace officer you need to understand that God never intended for you to be some "junk yard dog" that is required to be in attack mode all the time. As most of us know, it doesn't take much to set us off. We usually walk around wired all day, ready at a moment's notice, to unleash ourselves upon the public. We know what buttons we can push, and how far we can push them in order to invoke a reaction. However, can you imagine Jesus going around pushing people's buttons all the time? Had he been like that He would have never been effective in His work preaching, teaching, and spreading the "Good News".

As law enforcement officers, we all know about the use of the force continuum scale. It is a step-by-step process on how an officer should respond tactically to any situation. It starts with your presence and escalates up to and includes the use of deadly force. Did you know that Jesus knew when He needed to escalate on His force continuum scale? Jesus overturned money changers in the temple and chastised Jewish priests because of the way God's house of worship was being used. Read Mark 11:15. There will be times as law enforcement officers when we, like Jesus, will need to escalate our emotions as a way to help control a situation. However, we must make sure that our anger is directed toward the right issues and not just an emotional release.

Jesus also knew about having compassion as well. An aspect that many officers do not think about when putting on the uniform and badge. The Bible tells in Philippians 2:5 that our *"attitude should be the same as that of Christ Jesus"*.(NIV) Therefore, we need to throw away our stoic past and lead new Christ-like lives.

Small Group Scripture Reading- Read Romans 12:1-2 and discuss among your group how this verse can relate to your law enforcement jobs.

God Removes People in Authority

We believe that God uses governments and people in authority, like law enforcement officers and politicians, for His purpose. Since our authority is God-given, as described in Romans 13, we should be careful not to abuse or misuse it for our benefit. We are all too familiar with law enforcement officers who have gone bad and have been arrested, suspended, placed under investigation, and removed from their positions. When public officials abuse their authority they are not serving God's purpose and will be removed from their positions.

Small Group Reading – Read the following Bible verse as found in Daniel 2:21, *"He changes times and seasons; he sets up kings and deposes them. He gives wisdom to the wise and knowledge to the discerning."*(NIV)

There are other examples in the Bible where God has removed individuals from their positions of authority. Satan, once a Heavenly Angel named Lucifer, sat at the right side of God. He was removed and became a fallen angel for his sin and pride. This story is found in Ezekiel 28:14. Isaiah 40:23 tells us that God brings *"princes to naught and reduces the rulers of this world to nothing."* This is a pretty powerful description of God's authority.

Small Group Question & Discussion - Do you believe that Saddam Hussein and the country of Iraq could be one example of God removing a bad leader from a position of authority? Write below some other examples of individuals, co-workers, politicians, or celebrities that may have been removed from their positions of authority.

- _____

- _____

- _____

We can't be Judge and Jury

All too often law enforcement officers believe that it is okay to serve as both judge and jury. Some feel that they have the authority to issue out justice in accordance to whatever punishment they deem to be appropriate for the crime. Sometimes, while in the official performance of our job duties we can become consumed with the actions of individuals who we encounter; and may feel the need to take the law into our own hands. Let's face it; we all take crime and criminal activity very seriously, as we should. However, it is extremely difficult to keep from taking this criminal activity personally. For example, when someone gets a little resistant to arrest your emotions may take over and you may have the tendency to give them a "love tap" to slow them down.

We also tend to judge suspects by using words such as "crooks", "dirt bags", and "human garbage." Most cops reading this will think that these are only words tossed around to relieve the tension and stress of the job. However, it is important to remember that words such as these can lead to thoughts. Thoughts, once planted, can sprout up at the most inappropriate times such as following a pursuit or during a physical confrontation; or worse, such as when the media is nearby.

In every case where we allow our emotions to overtake us we are actually allowing sin to enter our minds at "Code 3 speed". It is when our physical and emotional state is at the highest that we allow Satan to control our thoughts and actions; often leading us right into a Federal courtroom for a Color of Law violation. During these times God is the furthest thing from our minds.

Now, allow me to be clear. I am not talking about self-defense. By all means you must protect yourself tactically against someone who has decided to take a violent action against you or that of your partner. But, we should never take the action against us personally. Slow down long enough to reflect on how God would want you to handle the situation. Whenever, we feel like we want to be both judge and jury we need to recognize that we are being tempted by evil. As Christians, we should cry out to God and ask Him to help lead and guide us in how to handle the situation as Jesus would. Jesus himself was tempted by Satan during his forty days in the desert as described in Matthew 4:1-11.

> ***Small Group Scripture Reading*** – Read the following Bible verse as found in 2 Samuel 22:7 (KJV) *"In my distress I called upon the LORD, and cried to my God: and he did hear my voice out of his temple, and my cry did enter into his ears"*

There are a number of officers, maybe some reading this study that have either been suspended or lost their jobs simply because they lost their cool and said something that they later regretted. The Bible teaches us in Romans 12:14-21 to hate the sin but not the sinner. Reading this passage can help keep us focused and help to maintain our sanity in a world full of sinners.

Small Group Scripture Reading & Discussion - Read the Bible verse as found in Romans 12:14-21 and then answer the following questions within your group setting.

- *How does reading verse 19 affect your thoughts about carrying out your job as a law enforcement officer?*

- *In verse 16 tells us to "not be proud". Do you find that we as law enforcement tend to exalt ourselves over others more often than not?*

The Faith of a Centurion

To often our faith is confused with our individual ability to attend church or worship God. While it is important to both worship God and align yourself with a church family, it is equally as important to have faith in God and His will for your life. Many people feel that they can have faith and not attend church. And many more attend church on a regular basis, yet don't have faith. In Luke 7:6-10, the Bible tells us the story of a Centurion (an Roman officer) who impressed Jesus with his strong faith. In order to be a successful Christian officer, like the Roman Centurion, more of us should use our faith in God while performing our job duties. Just imagine how God could use us for His purposes!

Small Group Scripture Reading - As a group read the Bible story of the Centurion with faith as found in the book of Luke 7:6-10. Then answer the following question as a group: Do you believe that you could possess the same faith as the Centurion did?

Small Group Scripture Reading – Read the following three Bible verses that address faith.

- Matthew 17:20, *"Because you have so little faith. I tell you the truth, if you have faith as small as a mustard seed, you can say to this mountain, 'Move from here to there' and it will move. Nothing will be impossible for you"* *(NIV)*.

- 2Corinthians 4:18, *"So we fix our eyes not on what is seen, but on what is unseen. For what is seen is temporary, but what is unseen is eternal" (NIV)*.

- Hebrews 11:6, *"...without faith it is impossible to please God" (NIV)*.

The bottom line is that you simply need to have faith in God through Jesus Christ, His son. You need to have the faith to believe that God wants to be a part of your life and to use you in your position as a peace officer for His greater purpose. If you feel that you have strayed off course in your search for a relationship with God, then maybe now is the time to redirect your life.

Chapter Three

Stress and the Family

"What Really Is Important"

Bible Verse: *"He who brings trouble to his family will inherit only wind, and the fool will be servant to the wise."* - Proverbs 11:29 (NIV)

Job versus Family

Ask any working professional what area of their life suffers the most and generally they will answer "my family life." Members of the law enforcement community are no exception and often their families suffer more from neglect and stress than the general population. As cops, we do some strange things to the ones we love because of the job. The shift work, weekend schedules, over-time and job stress of an officer can create a very hostile home life for their spouses and families. How often has your spouse had to re-arrange family functions to fit your work schedule or cancel the function because you picked up some extra over-time? Have you ever missed one of your child's school or sports functions due to work? Or better yet, when was the last time you just spent a nice relaxing day at home with your family or treated your spouse to dinner at their favorite restaurant?

Spouses of police officers are usually forced to assume a variety of roles within the family and often learn to function independently of their absentee loved ones. The families of officers can often have feelings of isolation and frustration. Spouses feel as if they have been left alone to raise the children and maintain a home life for someone they never see. Neglecting the things that God gives us like a family, is detrimental to the foundation of your family and your spiritual life.

My wife loves to tell the story about the night I proposed to her. It is a great example of how I fell into the trap of placing my job first. At the time, I was a Detective for the Sheriff's Department. The night of our proposal I planned a very romantic dinner. After dinner I was going to give her a ring and ask her to marry me. We had just finished our romantic candlelit dinner when my pager went off. I ignored the pager long enough to get down on one knee and ask her to marry me. After a few tender moments, where she thankfully agreed to marry me, I called the office to return my page. I was told that a tipster had called in to let me know that a fugitive, who I had been searching months for, was arriving in one hour on a flight from Texas and the airport was twenty-five miles away. So, I kissed my new fiancé goodbye and ended the night early. Why did I leave this romantic night? Because, the job called and everything else came second behind police work. Thankfully, my fiancé understood but in hindsight I was not setting a good precedent for the beginning of our new life together.

Ecclesiastes 9:9 says, *"Live happily with the woman you love through all the meaningless days of life that God has given you in this world. The wife God gives you is your reward for all your earthly toil." (NLT)* There will be milestone days in your marriage but the meaningless days outnumber them by a thousand fold. The key to living happily with your spouse is developing a servant's heart for him or her. Just as we serve God we should also serve our spouse. You need to care about the quality of his or her life and help them shoulder some of the responsibilities of organizing your home schedules.

Destructive Stress

Despite all the attention paid to the stress of a police officer's job, the fact remains that the most intense and destructive stress is the personal stress involving his or her own family. The intense encounters at work are usually occasional and short in duration. However, the stress generated by unresolved marital problems, family functions, money issues, and children's schedules makes for a corrosive element. If we let this control how we live our lives this can drain our ability to function effectively both on and off the job; and can cause detrimental cracks in the foundation of the family unit.

While there are no official nationwide statistics on divorce rates among law enforcement personnel, most experts agree that the estimates are as high as 75%.

It is important to note that this same destructive stress can cause us to neglect our spiritual family. Work, household responsibilities, and recreational activities can push us farther and farther away from the one thing we need the most, a relationship with God. It is simply a fact, whenever you are so overcome with personal issues we don't make time for anything else. It is then impossible for you carry out God's plans for your life. I know it seems that in times like these nothing else matters, including God.

God wants to be first in your life and He wants our families to prosper. We must learn to let Him take our anger, stress and frustration and replace it with heavenly peace. Matthew 11:28-30 states *"Come to me, all you who are weary and burdened, and I will give you rest. Take my yoke upon you and learn from me, for I am gentle and humble in heart, and you will find rest for your souls. For my yoke is easy and my burden is light.*" (NIV) And Ephesians 4:22-24 tells us to *"throw off your old evil nature and your former way of life, which is rotten through and through, full of lust and deception. Instead, there must be a spiritual renewal of your thoughts and attitudes. You must display a new nature because you are a new person, created in God's likeness--righteous, holy, and true."* (NIV)

It all comes down to how we prioritize. Letting the destructive stress of work and your family's hectic lifestyle take control of you will only cause further deterioration of the family's foundation. Placing God first in your life creates a strong foundation and a loving and nurturing home in which your loved ones can grow.

Small Group Scripture Reading – Luke 14:26 teaches us *"If you want to be my followers, you must love me more that your own father and mother, wife and children, brothers and sisters, yes, more that your own life."* (NIV)

Where is God in Your Marriage?

Try and think back to the day you were married. Do you remember the vows and commitments you made to your spouse to love, honor and cherish? You made these vows to not only your spouse but to God, in His house. The Bible teaches us in Numbers 30:2 that God wants us to always honor our vows to our spouse and to Him. *"When a man makes a vow to the Lord or takes an oath to obligate himself by a pledge, he must not break his word but must do everything he said." (NIV)* Many of us lose sight of the fact that upon marriage we were united as one with our spouse, placing personal gain aside and working as one in service to our Lord.

Place God first in your marriage by dedicating yourselves to reading His word and staying committed to following his laws. This will ensure a strong foundation for your family. In order to discover peace, fulfillment, and purpose within your marriage everything starts with a commitment to God.

THINGS TO REMEMBER!

- Keep God FIRST!
- Pray together
- Respect and honor each other.
- Encourage each other to grow together.
- Read the Bible together as much as possible.
- Attend Church services.
- Be swift to hear & slow to speak. Make time to communicate with each other.
- Protect and honor your marriage vows. Do not let others come between you.
- Thank God everyday for your mate & the life you have.
- Understand that "love" is a choice, not a feeling. Choose everyday to love your mate

Our Sinful Nature

We all know families who have been affected by destructive stress. Some of you are most likely working with other officers right now who are have marital and family problems, are separated or are already divorced. The absence of God in their lives has allowed a sinful nature to permeate their household and destroy the family bond. A few years ago, a female police officer in one of our PeaceKeepers groups related the following story. It is an excellent example of how sinful nature can creep in and undermine a happy home life.

This female officer was once married to another police officer who worked for the same agency. She was a 911 operator and her husband worked in the jail. While she was familiar with the job stress associated with law enforcement officers, she could never understand why her husband was always so moody and easily angered within their relationship. Finally, one night during an argument the husband shouted at her to "go sit on the curb!" She had no idea what this meant. Years later, after the divorce, she attended the Police Academy to become an officer. It was there that she learned that it was common practice for officers to tell their suspects to "sit on the curb" during street encounters; being used as both a control technique and a way to tell their suspects to calm down. In this particular case, the work stress in this officer overcame him and he actually began to treat his spouse as if she were a suspect. While at work you may be the main authority on your beat. However, you must be able to separate the stress of the job from your family. The officer in the above case could not.

The lack of respect exemplified in this story is just one identifying marker of sinful nature. Galatians 5:19-21 outlines other issues that can be just as detrimental to a marriage if not dealt with. *The acts of the sinful nature are obvious: sexual immorality, impurity and debauchery; idolatry and witchcraft; hatred, discord, jealousy, fits of rage, selfish ambition, dissensions, factions and envy; drunkenness, orgies, and the like. I warn you, as I did before, that those who live like this will not inherit the kingdom of God."* (NIV)

As Christian officers we should remember to be respectful to our spouses and our families by not allowing our own sinful nature to take control. 1 Peter 3:7 says *"You husbands must be considerate of your wives...Remember that you and your wife are partners together in receiving God's blessings."*

Small Group Questions and Discussion - Answer the following questions and discuss honestly among your small group.

- *Could you have forgiven your spouse if he or she told you to "go sit on the curb"?*

- *Have you ever, in a moment of anger treated your spouse as if he or she were a suspect?*

- *Have you ever used police lingo or terminology common only to those in law enforcement with your family?*

- *What can you do to overcome treating your spouse like a suspect?*

- *What can you do to avoid bringing home the stress of the job?*

- *As a law enforcement officer, I tend to treat people who I encounter at work with more respect than I do with my own family.* **Circle one: True   False**

Practicing the Fruits of the Spirit

If you were to list the character traits of your ideal mate what would they be? Would you want someone who is honest, faithful, joyful, patient and kind? Of course you would. No one sets out in life looking for a mate who is hateful, immoral and impure. The Bible teaches us that as Christians we are to strive to be Christ-like and allow the Holy Spirit to work through us. By doing so we will develop the character traits or the "fruits' of the Holy Spirit which will help us to defeat the desires of sinful nature. Galatians 5:22-26 tells us that the fruits of the Spirit are *"love, joy, peace, patience, kindness, goodness, faithfulness, gentleness and self-control. Against such things there is no law. Those who belong to Christ*

Jesus have crucified the sinful nature with its passions and desires. Since we live by the Spirit, let us keep in step with the Spirit. Let us not become conceited, provoking and envying each other." (NIV)

Having a successful marriage is dependent upon whether or not we develop the fruits of the Spirit within our families. But how do we do this? Simply stating that you want to be faithful and kind will not work. It all comes down to practice. Even as children we lacked patience and self-control. Through the guidance of our parents we were taught how to acquire these traits. The same goes now in our adulthood. The teachings of our Heavenly Father show us how we can emulate the fruits of the Spirit in our everyday life.

The Bible tells us to practice these qualities:

1. Practice being compassionate in your home.
2. Practice being kind to each other.
3. Practice being humble and giving others their way.
4. Practice being gentle with the words we say.
5. Practice being patient with the entire family.
6. Practice communication with your family and spouse
7. *Forgive* whatever your family member, co-worker, (or anyone else) has done to you.

Small Group Discussion – Faithfulness – One of the fruits of the Spirit outline in Galatians is faithfulness; a cornerstone trait in a successful marriage and spiritual life. There are four commitments that develop your faithfulness. Fill in the blanks below and then discuss the commitments within the group. The answers are found at the end of this chapter.

- Make a commitment to _____ in my _____.

"Be faithful to your own wife, just as you drink water from your own well." – Proverbs 5:15

- Make a commitment to _____ in the _____.

"Help, Lord for the godly are no more; the faithful have vanished from among men" – Psalm 12:1

- Make a commitment to _____ in _____.

"Give honor to marriage, and remain faithful to one another in marriage. God will surely judge people who are immoral and those who commit adultery" – Hebrews 13:4

- Make a commitment to _____ what God has given

"Now, a person who is put in charge as a manager must be faithful" – 1 Corinthians 4:2

After reading the above four steps to developing faithfulness, what is the one "recurring" theme or word in the above steps that stands out to you? Why do you think that _____ is important to being and staying faithful to God and your spouse?

Forgiveness

Even though as Christians we strive to be Christ-like, we still have the capacity to sin. We have to choose everyday not to give in to its temptation. And the Bible teaches us that when someone has sinned against us we should forgive them. Luke 6:37 states *"Do not judge, and you will not be judged. Do not condemn, and you will not be condemned. Forgive, and you will be forgiven."* (NIV) Sometimes this is easier said than done. It may be easy to forgive a spouse for not running an important errand or for forgetting your anniversary. But how do you forgive a spouse that does something as painful as committing adultery? God wants us to learn to forgive each other just as He forgives you everyday. God has formed a covenant with us through the death of His son, Jesus Christ, who died so that our sins would be forgiven. So, if God can forgive the person who sinned against you; is it to much to ask that you forgive them also? Matthew 6:14-15 also teaches us that *"if you forgive men when they sin against you, your heavenly Father will also forgive you. But if you do not forgive men their sins, your Father will not forgive your sins."* (NIV) It is important to note that forgiveness is not the same as trust. Forgiveness is given but trust is earned. You should always strive to work out the conflict that has occurred in your marriage and then do the things necessary to rebuild the trust.

Small Group Scripture Reading and Discussion – Review Luke 6:37 and Matthew 6:14-15 and discuss your answers to the following questions:

- *Who has committed a sin against you that you have not forgiven?*

- *What sins have you committed that you would like to have forgiven?*

- *What do you find the most difficult about forgiving others*

Relating to your Children

Throughout this chapter we have learned what stress and sin can do to our marriage. These detrimental effects can also be passed on to our relationship with our children. All too often, families in crisis blame the brunt of the family's problems on the children. I can't begin to recount how many calls for service involving runaway children that I rolled on. Most of the time I couldn't blame the child for running away from such a terrible home-life. I remember one family in particular. There were two daughters who were the product of their mother from a previous marriage. Then there were two sons from the father, also the product of a previous relationship. It was the second marriage for both parents and it was my third trip to their house. Make no mistake about this household it was no episode of the "Brady Bunch". One son was on Ritalin and had anger issues. One daughter was combating bulimia. The sixteen year old son was in juvenile jail for burglary. And I was being called because the second daughter had run away from home. The parents were extremely angry and, during the time that I was in their home, I witnessed them repeatedly yell at their other two children. At some point in the process of taking the police report, I asked them if they had a minister or someone from their church that I could call for them. They both looked at me and said "Why, what for?" With as much police politeness that I could muster, I told them that it was obvious to me that they had family issues that needed some-type of strong foundation other than what they were getting in their present home environment. I figured, "okay here comes the complaint." Instead, they both looked at me and said "you're right, we don't attend church." I left them with the names some chaplains and a few churches, including my own home church. I never saw the family at my church and I don't know if they ever attended another church. But I saw the opportunity to try and make a spiritual impact in the lives of these people who clearly needed God.

Ironically, pastors and law enforcement officers are constantly criticized for having the worst kids. Why do you think this is? Maybe they believe that their children will follow the straight and narrow in a strict, rule-driven home. Or, perhaps they think that the child will get the knowledge that they need through the benefit of osmosis by living in the same house as the righteous parent. But it does not happen that way. There is nothing stronger than a bond between a parent and a child. Why is it then that we take this special bond for granted? Having a strong, loving marriage will help to set the stage for a child's positive development later on in life. But we must also cultivate the relationship that we have with our child by loving them unconditionally; just as God loves us. 1Corinthians 13:4-7 tells us *"Love is patient and kind. Love is not jealous or boastful or proud or rude. Love does not demand its own way. Love is not irritable, and it keeps no record of when it has been wronged. It is never glad about injustice but rejoices whenever the truth wins out. Love never gives up, never loses faith, is always hopeful, and endures through every circumstance."* (NIV)

We, as parents have an obligation to God to raise our children in the way that He commands. Proverbs 22:6 tells us *"Train a child in the way he should go, and when he is old he will not turn from it."* (NIV) And Ephesians 6:4 states *"Fathers, do not exasperate your children; instead, bring them up in the training and instruction of the Lord."* (NIV) God loves us as His own children. He instructs us and guides us through His word so that we may prosper. Why then would we not do the same for our children? God's own son was sent here on Earth to be an example for us in how we should live our lives. Why then would we not try to set an example for our children through our actions? Parents, never abandon your Godly responsibilities to your children. Officers, never put the job and shift work ahead of your family's best interest. Never create stress or allow the stress found in your job to enter the sanctity of your marriage or your family. You owe it to both them and to God.

SOME HELPFUL TIPS FOR
A STRONG CHRISTIAN HOME-LIFE

- **Have Peace:** Allow God to give your home a peaceful atmosphere. Peace does not rely on circumstance but is a decision of your part that rests in your heart. How can your heart be at peace? Get God's word into your heart. The word will teach you and give you wisdom!

- **Worship:** Take time to sing and worship God every day. Christian Music can heal a stressed-out heart. Get connected. Attend a worship service or participate in a small group as much as possible. Get your children and your family involved in Church.

- **Be Thankful:** Be grateful and thankful to God for what He has already done in your home. When we constantly focus on the negative we forget what good things God has already done!

- **Give God Honor:** What ever you do, remember to always bring glory and honor to God.

- **Make Commitments:** Make a commitment to work together as a family. Every member has a responsibility to bring peace and unity into the home. As we all do our part stress will leave and peace, love, and joy will come rushing into our homes.

- **Love:** Love your spouse and speak gently to him or her. A husband (or wife) should never start flirting with another women (or man), and should never stop flirting with their own spouse.

- **Children:** Finally, parents should not expect children to make adult decisions. Remember when we were teens, we made dumb mistakes. Why? Because we were kids! When they blow it, forgive them and continue to teach them right from wrong. Don't expect children to know things when you don't take the time to teach them?

ANSWER KEY FOR
STRESS AND THE FAMILY

1. **PURITY** in my **MARRIAGE**

2. **INTEGRITY** in the **WORKPLACE**

3. **LOYALITY** in **RELATIONSHIPS**

4. commitment to **MANAGE** what God

5. Small Group Question to recurring theme is

COMMITMENT

Chapter Four

Carrying Out Our Christian Duties

"Understanding Our Purpose as Law Enforcement Officers"

Bible Verse: *"Go into all the world and preach the good news to all creation"* - Proverbs 27:17

As law enforcement officers we all entered our career with the idea of wanting to help people. We all envisioned being some sort of a superhero keeping them safe from criminals and being of service in times of need. Just think back to your first police oral board interview when you were asked the question, "So, why do you want to be a police officer?" And you, like thousands of other law enforcement professionals, answered "Because I want to help people." So, what happened in your career that has changed your heart and attitude? Why are so many law enforcement officers depressed, suicidal, divorced, and stressed out? I believe it is because we have lost sight of the primary purpose for our job. We are in law enforcement to be of service to our fellow man and this includes providing spiritual assistance when needed. Read Proverbs 27:17 above.

If you thought that the job description of a police officer involved looking cool in a uniform, driving fast with the lights and siren on, and telling people what to do, then you are in the wrong career. This is a very shallow way of thinking. Being a cop isn't all about fulfilling our own needs and desires. God has placed us on the front line in the war against good and evil. We are the protectors of humankind. Unfortunately, our job requires that we remain neutral in the way we enforce our laws. . However, you must not allow the neutrality of the job to get in the way of your ability to make a spiritual difference in the lives of the people that you encounter. No matter how you feel at the moment about your co-workers, law violators, or the complaints of the general citizenry; we must remember that they are God's people. And one of these individuals may need to hear God's "Good News" possibility for the first time in their life. Remember, you may be just the person God has chosen who can lead them to a life with Christ.

In Chapter One, we briefly discussed how God has given each of us unique skills and abilities to do our job. I think we can all agree that not just everyone has what it takes to be a cop. God is the ultimate chess player; assigning each of us with our own unique skills in just the right place at just the right time. Rest assured that God has plans for you. The bigger question really becomes, will you allow God to use you in your position as an instrument for His purposes?

Small Group Scripture Reading – Ephesians 2:10; *"For we are God's workmanship, created in Christ Jesus to do good works, which God prepared in advance for us to do.*

Authority and Respect

As Christian peace officers we have a responsibility to be on our best behavior in order to show Christ's love through our actions. Titus 2:7 teaches us *"In everything set them an example by doing what is good." (NIV)* No one should ever doubt that as a law enforcement officer you command authority and respect. After all, you represent the government. There have probably been many times during your career where you have doubted people's respect for you. Especially when we are spit upon, called vulgar names, physically beat up, and die in the line of duty while protecting and serving. However, the fact remains, that you are respected and people do listen to you. Did you know that even the President of the United States will stop what he is doing and listen to his Secret Service Agents? Why? Because even the President recognizes that those Agents have his best interest and that of his family in mind.

Although you may carry a badge, a firearm, and the authority of your agency, you are foremost a human being and a creation of God. In Genesis 1:26-27 (NIV) the Bible states, *"So God created man in his own image, in the image of God he created him; male and female he created them."* It is important to remember that while you command respect as an officer, you should not demand respect. Don't ever doubt or misuse your God given authority. As officers of the law we need to recognize that we are placed in a position of authority to make a difference in the life of someone with whom you may encounter. That someone could be a citizen or a criminal who you have arrested. It could be your supervisor or it may be the Chief of Police. It could be the Mayor, the Sheriff, or a fellow officer. Perhaps, it could even be the President of the United States. How you carry yourself, and what you say to others can speak volumes about the type of Christian you are. Let your Christian actions toward your fellow man reflect how God is working in your life. Philippians 2:5 states *"your attitude should be the same as that of Christ Jesus."* (NLT)

Loving Others

Throughout the Bible there are numerous references to the love that Christ showed for those who were sinners. Romans 5:8 says *"But God demonstrates his own love for us in this: While we were still sinners, Christ died for us."* (NIV) And John 13:1 states *"Having loved his own who were in the world, he now showed them the full extent of his love."* (NIV) As human beings we find loving people unconditionally very difficult. The Bible tells us in John 15:12 that Jesus commands us to love one another just as he does us. He is not talking about a physical love but rather a spiritual love. But don't worry. As law enforcement officers you can have a Christian spirit of love and still carry out your job duties. In fact, if more of us carried out our duties in a spirit of Christian love there would be less controversial arrests and suspensions for use-of-force violations. As Cops we would begin to not take words said or actions taken against us as a personal affront. It sounds so simple but we have allowed the criminal element on the streets to jade us and judge people and their actions.

We can often find ourselves questioning how God can forgive and love serial killers, rapists and child molesters. God hates the sin that these individuals have committed and has ordained law enforcement officers to arrest those who break the law. Romans 13:4 says this about an officer, *"For he is God's servant to do you good. But if you do wrong, be afraid, for he does not bear the sword for nothing. He is God's servant, an agent of wrath to bring punishment on the wrongdoer."* (NIV) But if the sinner repents and asks God for forgiveness it will be granted. God still loves them for the individual that they are. He loved all of us so much that He made the ultimate sacrifice so that our sins could be forgiven. The Bible tells us in John 3:16; *"For God so loved the world that he gave his one and only Son, that whoever believes in him shall not perish but have eternal life."* The spiritual lives of our fellow citizens should be of the utmost important to us. Because every lost person is important to God. And He has commissioned us to go out into the world and spread His good news of salvation.

Growing up as a youth at my Church in the 1970's there was a contemporary 'Jesus song', as they were referred to back then, entitled "We are one with the Spirit". You may remember it. The lyrics were *"We are one in the Spirit; we are one in the Lord. We are one in the Spirit; we are one in the Lord. And we pray that His unity will one day be restored. And they'll know we are Christians by our love, by our love.* The last line in this song explains what we should do in our quest to lead others to turn their lives over to God. We should show the world that we are Christians by our love. The same love that Christ showed to each of us when He died on the cross for our sins. Do not have hatred in your heart for sinners and evil doers. Instead, pray for them with all your heart that God will intervene in their lives. If the opportunity arises, share how God has worked in your life and show them you are a Christian by your love.

There are three Bible verses that instruct us in how to be a living example of Jesus Christ's love. As a group take turns reading the following Bible verses;

- Matthew 5:10 - *"In the same way, let your light shine before men, that they may see your good deeds and praise your Father in heaven."* (NIV)

- John 13:15 - *"I have set you an example that you should do as I have done for you."*

- Mark 16: 15-16 - *"He said to them, Go into all the world and preach the good news to all creation. Whoever believes and is baptized will be saved, but whoever does not believe will be condemned."*

Small Group Scripture Reading - Read 1st Peter 3 15:16 which states the following, *"Be ready at all times to answer anyone which asks you to explain the hope that you have in you. But do it with gentleness and respect."*

Let me be perfectly clear with this point; I do not expect you to stand on some street corner in full uniform and preach the gospel. Nor, would I expect you to have a prayer session with every person who you stop for a traffic violation. If you did these things then you would never be effective in your position as a police officer and it would cause to much negative attention on Christianity as a whole. However, here is what I believe God would expect from you. Every time that someone asks a question, be ready to give an answer.

For example, if you find a grieving person or the victim of a crime, take the time to speak or pray with them. Don't be afraid to offer to call them a minister or chaplain of their choice. We are dealing with a spiritually lost society who doesn't think about turning to God until they are deep into the worst time of their life. So, when you offer to call a spiritual leader for them you will probably get the same answer that I repeatedly got which is "I don't attend a church;" or, "Do you know a Pastor we could speak with?" Take this opportunity to invite them to church or offer to pray with them.

God opens doors and places people in our path for a reason. But, most of us miss this calling to make a spiritual impact simply out of fear of what others may think about us. Or else, we may dismiss it as preaching on duty. When we think like this we couldn't be further off the mark. To be a Christian also means to step outside your comfort zone. It also means that you have the faith that God will lead and guide you to make the proper statement at just the right moment in someone's life Never forget that God works on His time frame and not ours. Just because it is not a convenient time for you to tell others about your spiritual faith

Small Group Scripture Reading - Read the following Bible verse from James 2:8 *"If you really keep the royal law found in Scripture, "Love your neighbor as yourself," you are doing right."*

doesn't mean that God will say, "I'm sorry, maybe you can handle this some other time for me." You have to think more like a spiritual SWAT officer, ready to respond to a crisis at any time day or night. And that crisis may come at a moments notice and without warning

As law enforcement officers, one of the first things that you can do to love others is to begin seeing people through a different set of eyes; not through the cynical, distorted lens of police work. We should be viewing co-workers and citizens whom we encounter as individuals who God places in our path for a spiritual need. Read 1 John 4:19: *"We love because he first loved us."* By doing this, we can meet their needs by listening to their stories, working for their complaints, and going above and beyond the call of duty on their behalf. It is important that we love people in the same way that God loves us. We should not criticize, blame, unfairly judge, or turn a blind eye towards others. Because Jesus Christ would never have done that.

Are We Police Missionaries?

We are all familiar with church missionaries to foreign countries. They work in the poorest of countries throughout the world doing the work of Jesus Christ and serving the needs of many. Missionaries get very little pay. They work in the cold, rain, and heat; and work in natural disasters like floods, earthquakes, and tsunamis. They see famine, war, and death, and are often killed and placed into harms way in order to proclaim the good news of Jesus Christ. Tell me, what other occupation does this sounds like?

No matter if you are in a foreign land, in some part of the inner city, a rural country area, or in a jail setting; as a law enforcement officer you are in a mission field consistently being exposed to people around you with needs. How many of us miss this calling out of a personal pre-judgmental attitude? How many of us see the need but do nothing or else brush it aside saying "not my problem." The fact remains, that our desire to remain neutral in the enforcement of our laws has killed our spirit for helping others. However, our ability to identify the needs of others has nothing to do with carrying out the enforcement of laws. We should do our job as God commands. But, do not miss an opportunity to make a spiritual difference in your life or the life of someone else.

Small Group Exercise - Discuss among your small group the following ideas. See how these ideas can fit into your daily routine.

- Ask God to transform the way you think and help to remove your "rose-colored glasses". Romans 12:2 states the following: *"Don't copy the behavior and customs of this world, but let God transform you into a new person by changing the way you think."*

- Make a declaration of dependence on God. John 15:5 says, *"I am the vine: you are the branches. If a man remains in me and me in him, he will bear much fruit; apart from me you can do nothing."*

- Always worship and praise God even while on duty. Remember that worship is a lifestyle of loving God.

Small Group Discussion - What are some of the different ways we can worship God while on the job? Write a few examples here;

- _____

- _____

- _____

Small Group Question – Answer and discuss among your group the following question. "Do you believe that God has a plan for your life?" In what ways do you think God would want you to serve His Kingdom as a law enforcement officer? Write your answers below and discuss your answers as a group.

- _____

- _____

"Staying In Spiritual Shape"

In law enforcement it is important to be in physical shape in order to face any number of circumstances in which we could find ourselves. But how many of us ever think about staying in spiritual shape as well? Just as an unhealthy lifestyle will make you physically sluggish so can living an unbalanced spiritual life make you spiritually sluggish. 1 Timothy 4:7(b) says; *"Take the time and the trouble to keep yourself spiritually fit."* In order to stay spiritually fit it is important to read your Bible daily, pray constantly about everything, attend a worship service whenever possible, and get connected to a group of believers. It is extremely easy for those of us involved in the criminal justice system to become bitter. After all, we are on the front lines of life's failures. However, we must all BOLO (be on the lookout) for having this unresolved bitterness which can cause us to have deep resentment, and anger towards the public we are employed to serve. Hebrews 12:15 says we should, *"Watch out that no bitterness takes root among you, for as it springs up it causes deep trouble, hurting man in their spiritual lives."*

A Code of Biblical Ethics

The majority of all law enforcement officers are required to attend ethics training at least once a year. These ethic classes teach us how we, as government representatives, should act in a professional manner while addressing a variety of different scenarios. But how many of us have ever thought about having a code of Biblical ethics? God has given us an ethics manual in the form of the Bible that guides us and tells us how we should live our daily lives. Many officers have become jaded and their spiritual lives tarnished because of their dealings with the general public. They have become spiritually "blind" to the mission that God gives each of us that is to reach people for Christ. Many of us do not view these citizens as people who may have needed a spiritual shoulder to lean on. Instead, we have cast them aside; in effect telling them "Sorry, I don't have time to talk with you now, go see your Minister."

Romans 12: 14-21 could easily be a code of ethics for those in law enforcement. In the words of Paul, *"Bless those who persecute you. Bless and do not curse. Rejoice with those who rejoice, mourn with those who mourn. Live in harmony with one another. Do not be proud, but be willing to associate with people in low position. Do not be conceited. Do not repay anyone evil for evil. Be careful to do what is right in the eyes of everybody. If it is possible, as far as it depends on you, live at peace with everyone. Do not take revenge my friends, but leave room for God's wrath, for it is written, I t is mine to avenge; I will repay, says the Lord."*

Small Group Questions – Answer within your group the following questions.

- Do you as a law enforcement officer believe that the above Bible verse is applicable to today's modern law enforcement officers? If so why?

- Paul teaches us in Romans 12:20-21; "*if your enemy is hungry, feed him. If he is thirsty, give him something to drink. In doing this you will heap burning coals on his head.*" What do you believe the statement "*in doing this you will heap burning coals on his head*" means? Discuss openly with your small group.

-

Small Group Question - Write some examples of the times that you have become bitter while on the job. It could have been a missed promotion, a disagreement with a partner, a way of talking to a citizen, etc. Share your answers with the group.

- _____

- _____

- _____

Small Group Project - Take the time to identify your **"Most Wanted"** Write in the following spaces the names of three people that you would like to see come to Christ through your influence. These names could be co-workers, friends, family, or neighbors. Share them as a prayer concern with the group. Take the time to pray each day for those that you write down.

    1. _____

    2. _____

    3. _____

Some Practical Tips to Reach the Un-Churched

1. *Identify* – your surroundings. This includes your community, your small group of friends, relatives, neighbors, and fellow officers, or co-workers.

2. *Testify* – Testify on what God has done for you. Remember that people can always challenge the Bible, doctrine, or theology itself, but they can never challenge your our personal walk with Christ.

3. *Listen* – A great recipe for evangelism is two parts listening, one part speaking. Always be prepared to share your experience in this area. No one can dispute how God has impacted your life.

4. *Live It* – Allow yourself to be seen as a Christian. In other words, practice what you preach. Read the Bible as often as you can. Listen to Christian / Gospel Music. Pray and take the opportunity to talk with God often not just when you need him. Talk with Him all the time as you would a friend.

Chapter Five

God's Purpose For Our Work

"Do You Have a Pre-occupation with Your Job?"

Bible Verse- *"Whatever you do, do your work heartily, as for the Lord rather than for men, knowing that from the Lord you will receive the reward of the inheritance. It is the Lord Christ whom you serve." - Colossians 3:23-24*

A Misunderstanding of Work

Since biblical days, man has greatly misunderstood God's intent for our work. Many of us have allowed work to be our "god" (note the small "g"). We have come to expect a certain level of income and a material standard of living that we don't want to give up for anything or anyone. Sometimes, we throw ourselves into our work as a way to avoid problems at home or in our spiritual life. I have known officers that purposely work overtime every Sunday because they don't want to have to attend church with their spouse or family. I have spoken with other officers who told me that because they were forced to attend church between the ages of 8 and 18, that they no longer feel a need to give anything back to God. These officers believe that they have already completed their mission for the Lord and are now ready for early retirement from the Lord's service. Still others treat their worship to God as if it was some second job; working for free and get nothing back in return. For other officers, work is an excuse to avoid one's own spiritual hurting. No matter the reason, we need to understand that work is not a means to an end. It can never replace our spiritual relationship with God.

As Christians, we have overlooked the fact that our jobs are gifts that God has provided to us. They are not just meaningless and trivial reasons to get out of bed every day. Instead of focusing on the negative aspect of our jobs we should learn to be faithful stewards of them because God has given them to us.

Are You a Workaholic?

Workaholic's are compulsive people who are obsessed with work. They share the same traits as other people with addictions, such as substance abuse and food dependency. However, the law enforcement workaholic is unique in that their obsession is supported by the employer through the endorsement of overtime work, basing promotions on work dedication, and encouraging special assignments. Many department heads admire this type of work ethic because it is often more cost effective to pay an individual's overtime salary than it is to hire additional employees. But most importantly, obsessive working can be both financially and professionally rewarding to the individual officer. This ideology has been so engrained into our culture that we even have coined a term for it; "climbing the ladder to success."

Some of you who are reading this may be saying to yourselves "I'm not a workaholic. I just work a few extra details and overtime shifts to help keep my family financially stable." So, let's put this in perspective by answering honestly to a few questions. How many of your child's sport or social engagements have you missed? Is your spouse constantly complaining that you are never home? Are you feeling stressed about your home life? How many extra details and overtime shifts have you worked in the past month? Are you beginning to feel that your family has forgotten about you? Do you find that duty seems to always call? Others of you may feel as though you are forced into the extra hours due to the nature of the job. You treat your job in law enforcement not only as a career but as a way of life. This is an easy trap to fall into. After all, being an officer means that you are on call 24 hours a day, 7 days a week. And unfortunately, you are always going to be "married" to a pager, cell phone, or a portable radio until the day you retire.

Whatever reasons you use to justify your workaholic attitude it is important to remember that being a compulsive, obsessive worker will never get you ahead. Work always begets more work. The poet, Robert Frost, wrote *"By working faithfully 8 hours a day, you may eventually get to be the boss and work 12 hours a day."* Even if you are successful in your career, you will be lacking in other areas of your life. You may be a very successful officer; but what kind of a spouse, father, friend and Godly servant are you?

Perhaps it is time to take a step back and look at your work habits from God's perspective. He desires for us to be like Christ and be engaged in productive pursuits, such as work. But when you serve only yourself, through your job, then the work has lost its meaning and value. While our culture tells us differently; the fact is our work is not validated by the size of our paychecks, but rather by how we can allow Christ to use us through our jobs. And thus the challenge for the Christian law enforcement officer becomes clearer. We must maintain a healthy balance in meeting the responsibilities to the job, our family, and most of all to God.

Small Group Scripture Reading and Discussion - Read the following Bible verse found in Matthew 6:24 and discuss your answers to the following questions within the group. *"No one can serve two masters. Either he will hate the one and love the other, or he will be devoted to the one and despise the other. You cannot serve both God and money."(LB)*

- After reading this Bible passage, do you believe that you can serve two masters? For example God and Work? Share your answers with the group.

- Have you ever thought about God allowing you to be a steward over your possessions? Share your thoughts with your small group.

- Do you believe that you are currently working heartily for the Lord rather than for men?

- Do you see yourself as a workaholic?

A Life of Work
(The Real Story of a Workaholic)

How many of us have heard about the businessman or politician who has dedicated his or her life to their careers only to be terminated from employment or voted out of office? How many of you know a law enforcement officer that worked for thirty years and then only days into retirement suddenly died? A few years ago, I worked with a Deputy Sheriff named Dave. Dave was one of the hardest working cops that I have ever known. Over the years, Dave worked in every assignment that the agency had. He worked the traffic division as a motor cop. He was assigned to the river and range unit, criminal investigations, court security, community relations, and prisoner transportation. He was also both a DARE and PAL instructor. After thirty plus years, Dave finally retired on a Friday. A huge departmental retirement party was scheduled for the following Wednesday. Unfortunately, Dave never got a chance to attend his retirement party as he died of a massive heart attack on Monday. Dave's final weekend wasn't spent with his family or in a church service. Where was Dave? He spends his final weekend working as a used car salesman. Dave just couldn't stop working. He loved his family and they loved him. But Dave could not let his obsessive "work spirit" slow him down. Personally, I don't believe that it was Dave's purpose to serve God by working his entire life for a paycheck. Dave left behind a grieving wife and two grown children.

Small Group Question - Discuss your answers among your small group.

1. Does anyone know any law enforcement officer(s) like Dave?

2. How many "Dave's" are in this small group right now?

TIPS FOR THE "WORK-A-HOLICS"

- Understand that rest is not spare time, it must be scheduled.

- Give your relationship to God first priority in your life.

- Periodically review why you do what you do.

- Try to simplify the material things in your life.

- Simplify your family life.

- Attend Church / Worship Services whenever you can.

A Healthy Work Balance

Allowing you to be preoccupied with work is not the will of God; nor does He want you to be lazy and unproductive. We all must achieve a balance in our lives where we can be productive in all of our pursuits. God wants us to be successful in all of our endeavors. Jeremiah 29:11 tells us *"For I know the plans I have for you, declares the Lord, plans to prosper you and not to harm you, plans to give you hope and a future."* (NIV) You can start living your life with Godly balance by putting your priorities in the following order:

1. God first
2. Your relationships
3. Your job

Take the time to make a schedule for yourself. Reflect on where most of your energy is being expended. First and foremost, allocate time for God. Each day spend a few moments to reflect on God's teachings. One day out of your week should be spent attending church. Because of your varied work schedules, this day may not be a Sunday. That's okay. Set aside one day to be your Sabbath. Exodus 20:8-11 says *"Remember to observe the Sabbath day by keeping it holy. Six days a week are set apart for your daily duties and regular work, but the seventh day is a day of rest dedicated to the LORD your God. On that day no one in your household may do any kind of work. This includes you, your sons and daughters, your male and female servants, your livestock, and any foreigners living among you. For in six days the LORD made the heavens, the earth, the sea, and everything in them; then he rested on the seventh day. That is why the LORD blessed the Sabbath day and set it apart as holy."*

Second, make sure that time for work and family is balanced. Once you are done making out your schedule, review it. Are you working too much during a specific week? Have you remembered to write down important family events? Most importantly, have you remembered to keep a day aside during the week to worship God? By prioritizing your life and placing God first in all you do, you will be prosperous beyond your expectations.

Small Group Reading and Questions - Read the following Bible verse from the book of Exodus 34:21 and answer the questions below. *"Six days you shall labor, but on the seventh day you shall rest; even during the plowing season and harvest you must rest."*

- *Do you get enough rest?*
- *What does this Exodus 34:21 communicate to you about rest?*
- *What ways can you guard against overwork?*

IN ORDER TO HELP PRIORITIZE YOUR LIFE
TRY THESE SIMPLE STEPS

- ***PUT GOD FIRST*** - Put Christ as the center of your life and work in everything else around Him. Make a daily habit of reading your Bible, listening to Christian music, and spending as much time as possible praying and just talking with God.

- ***FAMILY SECOND*** - Your earthly family is God's gift to you. They are there for support and to help you through both difficult and pleasant times. Begin to look at the small things that your family will say or do. It is the smallest pleasures in life that can bring us the greatest joys.

- ***FINANCIAL ORDER*** - Bring financial order to your house. You may find this shocking, but you don't bring stability and happiness to your home by working more overtime or by bringing home a bigger paycheck. The old saying, "the more you earn, the more you spend" is very true. Try to remember that "It's not my money but God's money." Personally, this statement works for me. Because it serves to remind me that God has entrusted us to be a financial steward over the gifts that He has provided to us. So, use that responsibility wisely.

- ***WORK*** - This should be your last priority. Many of us fail to understand this principle. We have been taught from very early in life that the harder you work, the better your life will be. And the more money you make the more prestige you will have in your life and career. But this is a misleading thought implanted in us by Satan. Guard against overwork and stress that can drive us away from a relationship with God.

Small Group Discussion - Read aloud and answer together. Write in your answers in the blanks

- *We_____God when we obey Christ in our work.*

- *Our work is to be _____with witness and worship.*

- *The best way to deal with workplace stress is by _____ in _____to God for the gifts and talents that he has given us.*

Remember, we are on this earth for only a short time. Make the most of it by living a life that Christ would want us to live. Don't live the life that Dave did. Don't die working for a paycheck or recognition. Take the time to enjoy all of the gifts God has given you, especially your family. God didn't put you on this earth to live for yourself. He put you here for a purpose, and that purpose is to help others come to know Christ.

> ***Small Group Tip - Remember the following for spiritual strength.*** *"A job is not merely a task designed to earn money. It is also intended to produce godly character in the life of the worker."* - Author Unknown

---

Serving Others

Now that we have discussed what our job is <u>not</u> for, we should focus on what our Godly duties are. The primary purpose of law enforcement officers is to serve others. We can do this in a number of ways that aren't necessarily found in our job descriptions. Over the years, I have known police officers who delivered meals during holidays to the homeless community. I have known officers who had driven homeless out-of-towners to shelters instead of looking for a reason to take them to jail. I have seen officers pray with victims of crimes. I heard about a group of officers who visited sick children in the hospital and while there passed out stuffed teddy bears to them. I know a group of law enforcement officers personally that actually minister to prisoners in jail off duty. There are numerous things that you can do to serve both God and your fellow man both on and off the job. But , the most important thing that you can do, and one that would have the most impact for Christ, is to use your law enforcement job that God has blessed you with as an opportunity to outreach those that need Christ's love the most.

In law enforcement, we are already in contact with the people who need to hear about God's love and salvation the most. To describe it in my best southern terminology, you are already "fishing in a stocked pond". Now, let me challenge you on this point. Don't let the fear of being labeled "A Christian" slow you down from your work for God. Try looking at your assigned patrol community as your mission field for Christ; then, for the rest of your shift try to view yourself as one of God's special representatives to the citizens in your area. God wants you to tell others about Him. We are directed in the book of Luke 16:15 *"Go into all the world and preach the gospel to every creature."* God doesn't direct only pastors, ministers, chaplains, or priests to this work. Instead, He is commanding each one of us to do this work. Having the responsibility to inform others about God and the Bible can be scary, even for the most seasoned Christian. It is not difficult but it does require us to step outside of our comfort zone. Don't be concerned. God will remain with you and place the words in your heart that need to be spoken to the right people at the right time. You just have to be willing to be used by God.

After working in law enforcement for the past twenty-years, I know first hand that cops like to get into their comfort zones. After all, I've been in that zone myself. But being a "Christian Cop" means more. It means that God has selected you for a greater role than simply serving yourself. Now, before you become frightened about what I am suggesting to you, allow me clarify. Nowhere did I tell you that you have to "Bible thump" someone over the head. Nor, did I tell you to stand on a street corner with a sign that reads "The End Is Near!" While this may be a true statement, the Bible in 1st Peter 3:15-16 gives us a clear direction for telling others about the "Good News" of Jesus Christ. *"Always be prepared to give an* *answer to everyone who asks you to give the reason for the hope that you have. <u>But do this with gentleness and respect.</u>"*

One of the biggest problems, not only with law enforcement officers but with most Christians in general, is that too many people feel that we are not qualified to lead a life to Christ. In today's society, government has specialized and compartmentalized our profession so much that we start believing that in order to accomplish our daily assignments we have to have someone else, or some special unit, to handle everything. For example, we have been taught that police work is handled by the police officers; putting out fires is handled by firefighters; saving lives is handled by paramedics; and saving souls is the job of ministers and the church. While this concept has "professionalized" our positions in the field of public safety, it has nothing to do with the fact that we are qualified to tell others about the spiritual joy that is in us as Christians.

You know, God doesn't have a "go to" list of specialized individuals or college educated theologians to handle His needs. He has commanded all of us to spread His word; that includes me and YOU. Simply thinking that someone else will do it is not good enough. 2 Corinthians 2:14 says *"But thanks be to God, who made us his captives and leads us along in Christ's triumphal procession. Now wherever we go he uses us to tell others about the Lord and to spread the Good News like a sweet perfume."* (NIV) God puts no one else, except you, in a specific encounter in order to make the best spiritual impact possible. But the type of impact that you make is entirely up to you and your "free will". For example, you may decide to shrug off the incident and jump back in your patrol car to handle a different call. Or you can view the incident as God placing you at a scene as His instrument to be used for His benefit and glory. If you feel that you haven't been used mightily by God as yet just hold on. Soon God will put you in the position that He needs you in as a way to help lead a life to Christ. Use this study to become prepared to serve God.

Small Group Questions and Discussion: Take a moment to write some examples of how you can share your Christian faith while on the job. Share your answers with your small group.

- _____

- _____

  _____

A Life with Christ

Maybe you have never accepted Jesus Christ as your personal Savior. If this is the case, and you have now decided that you want to give something back to your Creator, then here are some simple steps for you to accept Christ into your life. Bow your head, and sincerely recite the following prayer. *"Dear Lord, I know that I have sinned in the past, and please forgive me. I want you to be Lord of my Life in everything I do and say. Please come into my heart right now and make me into the kind of person that you would want me to be. Use me, and allow me to make a difference in the life of someone in my role as a peacekeeper for you. In Jesus' name Amen."*

Saying this prayer is the first step to a changed life. But simply saying this prayer is not going to keep you from being confronted by evil on a daily basis. In order to help combat any evil you will need to surround yourself with other believers. Galatians 6:2 tells us *"share each other's troubles and problems. And in this way obey the law of Christ."* If you are reading this study guide as part of a small group then you are already surrounded with other believers. Pray that God will expand your small group for His benefit.

Don't Go It Alone Without God

As Christians, it is unwise for us to "go it alone". You need to be connected to other believers through the "body of Christ" which is the Church. Find a Church that you will feel comfortable worshiping and learning in. Don't select a church simply because it is the one that all your friends attend or the one that your family has been going to for generations. Step out and visit many different churches. Select one where you feel welcomed and one that you would want to keep coming back to for worship. No matter what church you select, remember to follow the advice that Pastor Rick Warren wrote in his book, 'The Purpose Driven Life'; *"if you have ever walked out of a worship service and said, I really didn't get anything out of that service today. Then you went to Church for the wrong reason. It isn't about you. Instead it is about honoring God."*

When I first read this statement I thought that Pastor Warren was writing directly about me. When growing up as a teenager it was common practice for me to walk out of a church service and be critical about something (or nearly everything) that had taken place. I would feel that that the message didn't touch me or the songs were too long and out-of-date. I would busy myself in the middle of the service doodling or checking out how much money other attendees put in the collection plate. Reflecting back on it now, I was not focusing on the word of God. Instead, I was focusing on the ceremony of God. I believed that I was attending church for the benefit of my own soul. Instead, what I should have been doing was learning the word of God and learning what I could do to lead others to Christ. This is a trap that many believers fall into, believing that attending church is all about "feeding our own souls". Instead, we should view attending church as our time of worship and giving our time back to God for what He has given to us.

Small Group Exercise – Answer the following questions <u>True or False.</u>

Studying the word of God will cause us to grow spiritually. _____

Since we can worship God as individuals, it is not ever necessary to meet with our church _____

God does not expect His children to enjoy giving. _____

God does not want to hear our requests. _____

Tips to Stay Focused For a Life with Christ

1. <u>**Understand that each of us has an obligation to God**</u> and to the body of Christ (*which is the church*). Remember that each of us should have a *"servant's heart"* in order to provide a <u>"service"</u> back to God and not simply to have a Church is here to <u>"serve us"</u> attitude. **Above all else we must first give back to God!**

2. <u>**Learn to surround yourself with a Christian attitude**</u>. I realize that in our line of work that is not easy. Each of us is surrounded on a daily basis by evil. Keep God close to you in your daily walk while on the job. Pray silently to yourself or in the company of your fellow Christian law enforcement officers. Keep Christian / Gospel music nearby.

3. <u>**Make a pact with God**</u>. Write down a list of promises that you have made or will make to God and what things that you will turn over to him to work out and manage for your own "peace of life". For example, you may write the following; "Lord, I will turn over my job to your will." Or, you may write "God, please give me the strength to be a great husband and father." Or, it may be a financial debt that you want to turn over to God. It can be anything at all. Writing down a list of items helps you remember that God is always nearby and will never turn His back on us even when we are surrounded by evil

4.Develop a vision for your service. See yourself serving God through your service to others. This can be done in a variety of ways. For example; by honoring your fellow officers, by having an absolute level of honesty in your job, by faithfully serving the citizens of your police community. By becoming involved within your small group or church. Use this PeaceKeepers study as a way to give back to God. Start up your own study and reach out to other law enforcement officers that you may know.

ANSWERS FOR GOD'S PURPOSE IN YOUR LIFE

- We **GLORIFY** God when we obey Christ in our work.

- Our work is to **BALANCED** with witness and worship

- deal with workplace stress is by **GROWING** in **GREATFULNESS**

- **True** - Study God's Word so that we may grow spiritually healthy -1 Peter 2:2

- **False** – Romans 12:5 *"In Christ we who are many form on one body, and each member belongs to all the others"*

- **False** - God loves *"a cheerful giver"* 2 Corinthians. 9:7

- **False** - 1 John 5:14 **"**This is the confidence we have in approaching God: that if we ask anything according to his will, he hears us.

Michael Dye

Chapter Six
God's Money, Not Mine?

"Striving to be financially free for God"

Bible Verse - *"No one can serve two masters. Either he will hate the one and love the other. You cannot serve both God and money."* - Matthew 6:24

Money is a hot topic for everyone. It seems that most anyone is willing to accept some guidance in nearly every area of their life, except when it comes to the subject of money. It is in the area of finance that people can really become defensive. My pastor once said, while illustrating a sermon on the use of our money; *"If you want to see where someone's priorities are, just look at their checkbook."* meaning that the majority of people center their lives around the use of money. In this chapter, we will address some ways that you can put money on the "back-burner". While you re-arrange your spiritual and life priorities.

As we have learned thus far, the job of a law enforcement officer is stressful enough without having to take on additional responsibilities such as working overtime and special details that can take you away from both your family and that of your church family for extended periods of time. We must never forget that this is exactly what Satan wants for us. Satan will try to distract us from the important things of life, like our worship to God and our important family time by using tools like our material wants and desires. Once we allow the "sin of greed" to get hold of our desires for the material things of life we start thinking something like; "If I work overtime for the next six Sundays, then I can afford that Harley."

You see, no matter what the material item is, it is Satan's goal to want us as far removed from God as he can possibly get us. And if Satan can do that with the lure of easy overtime money, and we allow it to happen, then we have given into our own sinful desires.

Small Group Scripture Reading – As a group take turns reading Ephesians 2: 3-5. Afterwards, answer the following questions.

- Have you ever found yourself working too much overtime?

- Have you worked overtime and missed Church because of it?

- Have you worked overtime out of necessity or out of greed?

Palm Trees and Tropical Ocean Breezes

I once had the opportunity to experience this "sin of greed" first-hand. When I accepted my position in federal law enforcement, my wife and I left our home in Daytona Beach, Florida for the big city of Los Angeles, California. We were only casual Church attendees in Florida and didn't mind missing a weekend here and there. But once we arrived in Southern California we still did not take the time to look for a Church to become involved with. The reason for this was simply because I was too busy working in my new job. From July 2000 to October 2001 as part of my official law enforcement duties, I spent every weekend traveling from Los Angeles to Honolulu, Hawaii. The reason for this travel was because the local office that I worked for in Los Angeles supported our Honolulu office on a special security project which necessitated the need for our travel to Hawaii every weekend.

While growing up as a kid, I could only dream of going to Hawaii. Now I was going every weekend. Flying out of LAX on Saturday morning and returning on Sunday evening. For all this "hard work" I earned about eighteen hours of overtime pay, and had the opportunity to lounge on the white sands of Waikiki. I visited every tourist site that the island of Oahu had to offer, Pearl Harbor, Diamond Head, Waimea Bay and more. I was rolling in the money, and swaying in the island palm trees. And here was the best part. Since, I wasn't home on the weekends my wife did not want to be home alone either, so she worked overtime at her job as a Registered Nurse. Money was good for us. Never once did I stop to realize what we were missing in the form of a Church family. However, that was soon about to change. Little did I know that God had sent a guardian angel to us in the form of a co-worker by the name of Leon Lancaster. Leon kept inviting me to his church and I kept stalling. After all, I was busy flying to the islands every weekend and I really didn't have time for Church or for God. Finally, I had one weekend off when I wasn't traveling, and my wife wasn't working. So, more out of obligation to Leon than interest in "getting involved in some Church", my wife and I decided we would visit Leon's Church.

Needless to say it was a life changing experience. Because shortly there-after I quit traveling to Hawaii and instead my wife and I spent our weekend Sundays going to Church. The whole point in my story is this. My travels to Hawaii and earning lots of money caused both me and my wife to be distracted from God for well over a year. Eventually, I came to learn that the Lord had great things in store for us but, had it not been for my co-worker, Leon, inviting me every week to Church, I would have remained blinded by the lure of money, palm trees, and tropical ocean breezes.

You see, I believe God had a plan in the form of Leon and that was to lead my wife and I back to God. As a direct result of Leon inviting me to Church, you are now reading this study. Leon, just like each of us has a choice. Invite me to his Church once and leave it alone. Instead, Leon felt a calling to repeatedly invite and ask me. Leon understood what the Bible in 1 Corinthians 15:58 said; *"Therefore, my dear brothers, stand firm. Let nothing move you. Always give yourselves fully to the work of the Lord, because you know that your labor in the Lord is not in vain." (NIV)* God Bless Leon for his gift of persistency!

Financially Free for God

To be financially free is something that neither Satan, nor our credit card companies want for us. Becoming financial free really becomes a battle of "good versus evil." If given a choice, I believe that we would all like to become financially free in order to not have to work any longer or to be able to afford the many luxuries of life. However, God does not want us to be enslaved to money, possessions, or to our creditors. God would rather that we be financially free as a way to honor Him and not ourselves. Striving to be financially free so that we can spend more of our time giving back to God should be a goal for all Christians.

The Lust for Money

Many of us have the mistaken belief that God can be *"Lord of my life,"* but not *"Lord of my money."* We want to keep God separate from our money. But God never intended for that to occur. The Bible has over 2,350 verses that talk about money and possessions. That's more verses than God spoke about love or salvation. The Lord spoke so much about money because even 2,000 years ago, He knew that much of our lives would center on its use. Greed and the lure of money have caused more people to sin. Greed and the lust of money are what keep drug dealers in business. It is what keep our school children from wanting to learn and instead want to become a major league sports figure by the age of fifteen. Greed and the lure of easy money is why our jails are full of bank robbers, murders, con-artist, burglars, prostitutes, and thieves. And sadly, it is why many of us miss church and miss being connected to a group of fellow believers. Yes, money is a necessity but we should use it as such, and with great responsibility.

Small Group Question – Discuss openly with your group the following question

Write three items that interferes with your worship and service to God?

1. _____

2. _____

3. _____

Lord of my Wallet?

During the Crusades of the 12th century, the Crusaders hired mercenaries to fight for them. Because it was a religious war, the mercenaries were baptized before fighting. As they were being baptized, the soldiers would take their swords and hold them out of the water, to symbolize that Jesus Christ was not in control of their swords. They felt that they had the freedom to use their weapons in any way they wished. While we may not be as obvious about it as these soldiers were, many people today handle their money in a similar fashion. Many Christians hold their wallet, purse, credit cards, and checkbooks "out of the water" in effect saying, "God, you may be the Lord of my entire life, except in the area of money, in that area I am perfectly capable of handling that myself".

Whenever, we allow ourselves to think that we are capable of honoring God on our owe, we are sinning by setting limitations on God and just how much we are allowing him to be involved in our everyday life. We see this in the book of John 15:4 in which Christ instructs us; *"Remain in me, and I will remain in you. No branch can bear fruit by itself; it must remain in the vine. Neither can you bear fruit unless you remain in me".* God should be in every area of our life. Not just in some areas. Not just on Sunday but everyday and in every aspect.

> ***Small Group Question*** – Discuss among your group the following question. After reading the above paragraph and Bible verse, *"do you allow God to be Lord of your entire life, or just Lord of parts of your life?"*

If we cannot serve both God and money at the same time then why do we spend as much time working overtime as we do? Is it out of necessity, or out of greed that drives us to work? Or does our department demand? As Christian law enforcement officers we should be serving Christ through our unique profession and through the people that we encounter while in our jobs. We should not spend our efforts keeping God away from the possessions that He has blessed us with, and that includes our families. Instead, we need to learn to use the gift of our job to God's glory. Make the effort to attend church or a small group Bible study at least once every week. As the Bible in John 15:4 states; *"Remain in me, and I will remain in you. No branch can bear fruit by itself; it must remain in the vine. Neither can you bear fruit unless you remain in me."*

A big part of law enforcement work is the time that is spent away from the things that matter most. Such as time spend with the family, our spouse, our kid's activities, special occasions, Church, and the study of God's word. So, in this sense, money really becomes a primary competitor with Christ for the "heart of our worship." We need to be consistently reminded that God is the owner of all of our possessions and we are only the caregiver for the things that God has provided to us.

While this may seem easy to believe from a Christian's point of view, this idea is totally contrary to what our society tells us that we should do. Our culture, the media, and even our laws tell us that

---

- Debt is always a liability - *"Keep out of debt and owe no man anything." – Romans 13:8*

- Debt contributes to slavery - *"The poor are ruled by the rich, and those who borrow are slaves of moneylenders" - Proverbs 22:7*

- Debt leads to poverty - *Deuteronomy 28:15, 43-44*

- I live on credit, rather than paying cash - *"Don't withhold repayment of your debts. Don't say, some other time, if you can pay now." - Proverbs 3:27-28*

- I'm trying to keep up with my neighbors - *"I have also learned why people work so hard to succeed; it is because they envy the things their neighbors have. But it is useless. It is like chasing the wind." - Ecclesiastes 4:4*

- I fail to put God first in my finances - *"You people are robbing me, your God. And, here you are asking. "How are we robbing you? You are robbing me of tithes and offerings" - Malachi 3:8*

---

what you possess, you alone own. Read the following Bible verses about the possessions you own and after reading, see if it now gives you a different perspective

Small Group Scripture Reading – Take turns reading 1 Chronicles 29:11-12 (NLT); *"Everything in the heavens and on earth is yours, O LORD, and this is your kingdom. We adore you as the one who is over all things. Riches and honor come from you alone, for you rule over everything. Power and might are in your hand, and it is at your discretion that people are made great and given strength"*

Small Group Exercise - Read Matthew 6:24 as a group then answer the following questions;

1. *Do you believe that you can serve both God and money? If so, describe how.*

2. *In what ways can you keep a balance between family, church, and work? Share your answers with the group.*

Godly Business Leaders

Don't be frightened about God leading us in matters of our finances. Many great business and political leaders have placed God first in their business practices and it has turned out for the best. Here are some examples to look towards;

- **Truett Cathy,** owner and founder of the fast food chain "Chick-fil-a", went totally against advisors when he decided to honor God by keeping all 1,125 nationwide stores closed on Sundays. Today, "Chick-fil-a" is one of America's fastest growing fast food restaurants and is a major sponsor of LPGA, college football bowls, and NASCAR races. And yes, all stores are still closed on Sundays.

- **John D. Rockefeller**, one of the wealthiest men in American history, made his fortune all while holding onto this simple principle: the first 10% of all his monies went to God, the second 10% went to savings, and 80% went to expenses and spending.

- **William Borden** was a man born to be rich in the early part of the 20th century. He became the sole heir to a multimillion dollar estate, various silver mines in Colorado, and heir to the Borden Dairy Corporation. He graduated from Yale Business School, then against his father's wishes gave up "the good life" to follow Christ as a missionary to China. While at Yale he used his wealth to start up and finance the "Yale Hope Rescue Mission" that reached out to those who were down and out as well as spiritually lost. He graduated from Princeton Divinity School and went to Egypt in 1912 where he spent his time distributing Bibles and preaching among the sick and poor. While doing this work, he contracted meningitis and died at the age of 26. Just prior to his death on April 9th 1913 he summarized his thoughts on dying. While he never reached his goal of being a missionary to China yet his last words found in his Bible were written: *"No Reservations, No Retreats, No Regrets."*

- **U.S. President Harry S. Truman** once said: *"I do not think that anyone can study the history of this great nation of ours without becoming convinced that divine providence has played a part in it. I have the feeling that God has created us and brought us to our present position of power and strength for some great purpose"*

Small Group Exercise – Read each of the following statements on the three reasons to put God first in my personal and business finances;

- It's a statement of my **gratitude**
- Its a statement of my **priorities**
- It is a statement of **my faith**

Small Group Question - Answer and discuss the following questions together as a group.

- How many of us could give up our life fortunes and possessions for God?

- How can we honor God in our home financial practices just as these men have done in their business lives?

- How many of us can't find the time to give one day each week back to God?

Chapter Seven

Why Do Bad Things Happen?

"Why do bad things happen to good cops?"

Bible Verse – *"So don't be misled...whatever is good and perfect comes to us from God" – James 1:161-7 (Living)*

Why do bad things happen? This is by far the most difficult of all the "big questions" to answer. There is no easy answer to this question, especially when it has affected someone close to us. In fact, some people go so far as to turn from believing in God when something bad happens to them or to someone they love. They question God as to why He allowed something bad to occur. I believe that there are a couple of reasons for our questioning. First, most people don't have a strong spiritual foundation to understand that God doesn't "allow" bad things to happen to us and second, we don't want to believe that a benevolent and loving God could allow any type of suffering.

On the one year anniversary of the September 11th tragedy at the World Trade Center the PBS television show, 'Frontline' aired a television special survey about God and faith during the events of that day. Their survey showed that before "09-11" most people believed in a benevolent and loving God. After September 11th, most people had trouble believing in God at all. Their study showed that the individuals surveyed didn't want to believe that God could allow such a tragedy to occur. Many harbored resentment towards God for their personal suffering and lost. But suffering is not something that

God desires for us. The Bible in James 1:13 tells us; *"Don't blame God when you are tempted! God cannot be tempted by evil and he doesn't use evil to tempt others."* Instead, God gave mankind something called "free will". Because of man's free will, people can choose to follow a life with Christ, or follow a life with Satan into sin. But make no mistake about it God does hates the sin that man creates. In spite of this, the Bible in the book of Hebrews 13:5 tells us that God promises never to leave our side.

Small Group Scripture Reading –Hebrews 13:5 *"Never will I leave you; never will I forsake you"*

But as Christians, we can't forget that Jesus Himself knows what it is like to suffer. After all, He was persecuted, left hungry, tempted, mocked, beaten, had nails driven through His hands and feet, His side was pierced with a sword, hung on a wooden cross, and He went through it all including dying for our sins.

The Soul of a Cop

When it comes to the job of a law enforcement officer, there are a few things that can eat at the very soul of a cop and can cause officers to become bitter about the job. First, it is the guilty that go free. How distressing it is for us to pursue, arrest, and book a law violator only to see them back out on the street by the end of our shift. Second is the death of a fellow law enforcement officer, especially, when that officer was killed in the line of duty enforcing the laws and carrying out the duties that so many people take for granted. Another is the death of a child through tragic and needless situations such as abuse, neglect, or vehicle accidents. Generally speaking, law enforcement officers see both crime and tragedy day in and day out. They see death and dying, corruption and politics, they see distrust from citizens, they are spit upon, cursed at, and they see the worst of humanity towards one another. To me, this sounds a lot like what trials and suffering that Jesus Christ endured. So, as mere humans who are full of sin, it is little wonder why law enforcement officers can become so bitter and soured on the society that they are paid to protect. However, this is where we need to remember that Jesus Christ never became soured on society.

While watching the television news coverage of the case of Terri Schiavo in Florida I saw something directed towards a police officer that I found appalling. If you remember, Terri Schiavo was the woman in March of 2005 who was the focus of having her feeding tube disconnected by court order and in the process prompted both the President and Congress of the United States to become involved. As I watched the newscasts of the protesters outside of the nursing facility, I wondered to myself what those police officers who were guarding the nursing home must be thinking about all the Christian protesters when I saw a protester shout at a police officer saying "God hates you and you are evil!" I was shocked and disappointed. Here was supposedly, a "peaceful Christian" protester disobeying God's commands from Romans 13:1. At that moment, I wanted to reach inside the television set and tell that officer, "God doesn't hate you!" In fact, while many men hate God, there is no man that God hates". Romans 12:9 states; *"Love must be sincere. Hate what is evil; cling to what is good."* If there was anything that God would have hated that night it was the actions of the protesters not following His own rule of law found in Romans 13: 1-7. Additionally, in Titus 3:1-2 we are told *"Remind the people to be subject to rulers and authorities, to be obedient, to be ready to do whatever is good, to slander no one, to be peaceable and considerate, and to show true humility toward all men."*

Small Group Scripture Reading - Read together as a group the following Bible verse from Romans 13:1-7;

"Everyone must submit himself to the governing authorities, for there is no authority except that which God has established. The authorities that exist have been established by God. Consequently, he who rebels against the authority is rebelling against what God has instituted, and those who do so will bring judgment on themselves. For rulers, hold no terror for those who do right but for those who do wrong. Do you want to be free from fear of the one in authority? Then do what is right and he will commend you for he is God's servant to do you good. But if you do wrong, be afraid, for he does not bear the sword for nothing. He is God's servant, an agent of wrath to bring punishment on the wrongdoer. Therefore, it is necessary to submit to the authorities, not only because of possible punishment but also because of conscience. This is also why you pay taxes, for the authorities are God's servants, who give their full time to governing. Give everyone what you owe him: If you owe taxes, pay taxes; if revenue, then revenue; if respect, then respect; if honor, then honor".

I pray that the officer who was so wrongly shouted at by this protester did not have his faith shaken by those words. This incident should serve to show why a strong foundation in Jesus Christ is such a necessary part of a law enforcement officer's job. Using this officer as an example, assume for a moment that this officer did not have faith in God, or maybe he was an officer who might have been seeking God. After being yelled at by Christian protesters for three weeks straight, what do you think his thoughts about God and Christians are now?

Citizens forget that we in law enforcement are put into some difficult situations as part of our jobs. Often times, police officers, as part of their official duties are required to enforce laws that go against many of their own Christian beliefs such as arresting protesters at anti-abortion rallies, or, the 2001 case in Indiana where United States Marshals had to enforce a federal court order and seize a church for $6 million dollars in unpaid tax bills. But the inspiration that we should be looking for to keep us positively motivated for carrying out these difficult tasks is what the Bible says in Romans 13:verses1 and 2; *"Everyone must submit himself to the governing authorities, for there is no authority except that which God has established. The authorities that exist have been established by God. Consequently, he who rebels against the authority is rebelling against what God has instituted, and those who do so will bring judgment on themselves"*.

So, how do we deal with questions like, *"Why do bad things happen to good people?"* and *"How can God allow bad things to happen to great cops?"* These are not new questions. They have *been* asked by every generation of peace officer.

Small Group Question – Discuss among your small group the following question.

- What if any laws could you not enforce based upon your own Christian beliefs. If so why?

Small Group Scripture Reading – Read the following two Bible verses;

- James 1:13; *"When tempted, no one should say, "God is tempting me." For God cannot be tempted by evil, nor does he tempt anyone;*

- James 1:16-17; *"Whatever is good and perfect comes to us from God above, who created all heaven's lights. Unlike them, he never changes or casts shifting shadows"*

Job, God's Faithful Servant

When I think of questions such as these, I immediately think of Job. Job in his time had everything a man could want. He had a family, wealth, respect, health, and an extremely strong faith in God. And in a single day it was all taken from him.

> ***Small Group Scripture Reading*** - Take turns within your small group and read the following Bible verses. Job 1 verses 1-22, and Job 42 verse 12.

The Highlights of Job's Troubles

Just in case you may have missed it, here is a sample of what Job endured.

- *A group of terrorists attacked his servants, killed them all and stole all of his oxen and donkeys.*

- *Fire came down from the sky and consumed all of his sheep and all of the servants that were watching them.*

- *Another group of terrorists attacked and killed those servants who were watching his camels and they were all stolen.*

- *If that wasn't enough, there was a structural collapse of a building, and all of his children were killed (seven sons, and three daughters).*

- *Job was inflicted with boils and skin rashes.*

But in all of this, what was Job's reaction? sorrow and grief? yes, certainly! But in the midst of that grief he still was able to worship the Lord, saying, *"Naked I came from my mother's womb, and naked I shall return there. The LORD gave and the LORD has taken away. Blessed be the name of the LORD."* (Job 1:21).

Even after all that he went through, Job was still able to recognize that anything given to him was from the hands of God and that he was only a steward of the possessions that God had bestowed upon him. Job says, *"I came into this world with NOTHING."*

Small Group Questions - Read the following questions and discuss as a group your answers.

1) Could you have endured the same afflictions as Job did and Still praise God?

2) What "bad things" have happened to you? Did you blame God for your troubles?

3) Do you view yourself as being a steward of the possessions God has blessed you with?

Job Teaches Us a Lesson

There are a few things that Job knew about God that we should learn from. First, Job was patient with God. Why? How could he be so patient, you ask? First, because Job knew that God was patient with us. Many times during our own trials we become so wrapped up in our own suffering that we forget that God is even there with us. We focus only on our own pain that we are filling at the moment.

We cry out to God and ask why? But we are never patient with God. In fact, if anything we are impatient and curse God for placing us in that situation. Yet, in Deuteronomy 31:8, God tells us, *"The LORD himself goes before you and will be with you; He will never leave you nor forsake you. Do not be afraid; do not be discouraged."*

Second, Job knew what is found in 1st Peter 1:7 was true;*" These trials are only to test your faith, to show that it is strong and pure. It is being tested as fire tests and purifies gold, and your faith is far more precious to God than mere gold. So, if your faith remains strong after being tried by fiery trials, it will bring you much praise and glory and honor on the day when Jesus Christ is revealed to the whole world."*

Notice that we are told that these are "trials" not "temptations". There is a difference between the two. Temptation is when we are tempted by our own evil desires. The Bible instructs us not to blame God when we are tempted. This is found in the book of James 1:13 and says; *"Don't blame God when you are tempted! God cannot be tempted by evil, and he doesn't use evil to tempt others"*. The Bible in James 1:13-15 tells us the following; *"....each one is tempted when, by his own evil desire, he is dragged away and enticed. Then, after desire has conceived, it gives birth to sin; and sin, when it is full-grown, gives birth to death."*

God Uses Our Tragedies for His Benefit

I realize that this may be a difficult concept to accept. But, from time to time, God will take a step back from us, and allow us the opportunity of having trials. This does not mean that God wants bad things to happen to us and it doesn't mean that God doesn't love us. In fact it is quite the opposite of that. God uses times of trials to test our faith and as a way for us to learn that we can't make it alone in this world without having

God in our lives. However, God can use our tragedies to the benefit of both ourselves as well as others. For us, these tragic circumstances can give us the opportunity to learn and "grow to God". The Bible in James 1: 1-13; tells us to consider these trials as *"pure joy"*.

A great example of how can God work through us is the following story. Once, I was asked to host a home Bible study. There was a couple who were new to our Church and they were looking for a small group to connect with. They signed-up for our group simply because we were meeting close to where they lived. Also, in our group was a number of other couples and one of these couples, named Jim and Joann had lost their son years earlier when he was sixteen years old in a tragic vehicle accident. During our first small group session, as each couple were introducing themselves, our new couple mentioned they had just recently lost their twenty-five year old son to a road raged driver who was never caught. They also mentioned that they were angry at God for their lost, but they were now trying to spiritually cope with the tragedy. Needless to say, these two couples immediately bonded because of the tragedy that had occurred in both of their lives. There was no one better to minister to this new couple then Jim and Joann.

Was it *"simply luck"*, or just a *"coincidence"* that out of the dozen or more home study groups that were meeting in our area at that time, our group had someone else with a nearly similar tragedy? I would prefer to believe that it was the hand of God at work here. While

---

Small Group Scripture Reading – Read James 1:1-13 and discuss the following questions as a group. *"Consider it pure joy, my brothers, whenever you face trials of many kinds, because you know that the testing of your faith develops* perseverance. *Perseverance must finish its work so that you may be mature and complete, not lacking anything"*.

- Have you ever considered your trials and troubles *as "pure joy"*?

- Do you believe that God can speak to us during our trials?

---

everyone in our small group have became great friends. I know that these two couples developed an extra strong bond because of their similar tragedies. This is exactly what God wants. For Christian believers to support one another, and that includes Christian cops. God wants us to be connected to a group of other believers. He doesn't want us to try to *"self-cope"* with our struggles and He doesn't want us to be weighed down with our own self-pity. Instead, He wants us to go into action to help one another out in our difficult times. This is the essence of God's love manifested through us.

Small Group Scripture Reading – Read the following Bible verse from Ephesians 2:10; *"For we are God's workmanship, created in Christ Jesus to do good works which God prepared in advance for us to do"*.

Burnt Cookies, God's Lesson to Us

When my younger brother was around the age of five years old, he wanted a cookie that was in a batch that was burnt. Our mother repeatedly told him *"No,"* however, he kept on crying and insisting. So, what did she do? She allowed him to eat one of the burnt cookies. She watched him from a distance, as he spit it out and very cutely said, *"Yucky!"* Our mother was never far from him and she would have never let him eat the whole cookie, but she allowed him just a little bit of freedom to understand that he wouldn't want to eat a burnt cookie. It was a lesson learned.

I believe that God also does the same thing with us. We pray and we ask, and we want of God, but too often we don't even understand the consequences of what we are asking for. But God knows. He may not give us what we want or desire at that particular moment in time for other reasons known only to Him. But we need to trust and have faith that God is making the correct decisions for us. This goes directly to the heart of our spiritual faith with God. As Christians, we need to lay all of our burdens, struggles, and suffering before God. We need to pray and trust that God will always be with us during our times of suffering. Sometimes there are great answers found in prayer. Sometimes the answer is simply in knowing God's peace, joy, and help as we go through the suffering, and this in itself is what brings hope to others who see us as Christians.

As Christian officers, we can bring hope to those that need it most. And often, this can mean our fellow co-workers. It is in the difficult and stressful times of your career when you can really fulfill God's purpose for your life. Yes indeed, God does need first responders and you may have been placed in someone's difficult moment as an answer to prayer. Don't miss your opportunity to lead someone to a life with Christ, whether on or off-duty.

Small Group Reading - Take turns reading the following Bible passage from James 1:2-4- *"Is your life full of difficulties? Be happy, for when the way is rough, your patience has a chance to grow. So let it grow and don't try to squirm out of your problems. For when your patience is finally in full bloom, them you'll be ready for anything, strong in character, full and complete"* (Msg)

Being FIT for God

It is important to realize that God will never give us more than we can handle. Read the following Bible verses as found in 1Corinthians 10:13 (NIV) –*"No temptation has seized you except what is common to man. And God is faithful; he will not let you be tempted beyond what you can bear. But when you are tempted, he will also provide a way out so that you can stand up under it."*

We must all remember that God is always in control. Life is difficult at times. Good things and bad things happen to everyone. Becoming a Christian does not mean that your life will get easier. In fact, it will probably even get tougher. Satan attempts to make things more difficult for Christians because we are not afraid to share our faith with others. As a result, we have the largest opportunity to change lives for Christ. So, in this regard we often walk around with a big target on our foreheads for Satan. However, with that said, being a Christian and going through difficult times is a lot like exercising our bodies. When we first start a physical exercise routine, like running, it can be difficult, and our bodies become sore. However, with time, and mentally working through our pain we become stronger and more physically fit.

Being a Christian is very similar. Our pain makes us spiritually stronger. And as we become more "spiritually fit" through life struggles, so we may become spiritually stronger to assist others through their life difficulties. Never forget that being a Christian also means that you will have God to help you through every hard time. He is just waiting on you to call upon Him for help and guidance. But in order to experience this you must follow the Bible and its commands. Read Deuteronomy 6:4-5 *"The Lord is our God, the Lord is one. You must love the Lord your God with your whole mind, your whole being, and all your strength."*

Small Group Question / Discussion –

- Do you feel that you are now spiritually fit?

- Do you believe that you have the abilities to lead others to Christ?

Some Helpful Tips

- ***Release my grief -*** *Don't deny it or ignore it. Let God know exactly what you are feeling. Matthew 5:4 - Blessed are those who mourn".*

- ***Receive help from others*** *- Don't isolate yourself. Find support in a church family. "Carry each other's burdens" - Galatians 6:2*

- ***Refuse to be bitter -*** *You have a choice - become bitter or better "Some people have no happiness at all; they live and die with bitter hearts" - Job 21:2*

- ***Remember what's important*** *–"Relationships, not things, are what matter." - Luke 12:15*

- ***Rely on Christ -*** *This is the secret of strength in tough times. "I have learned the secret of being happy at any time in everything that happens; I can do all things through Christ, because he gives me strength." -* Phil 4:13

Michael Dye

Chapter Eight

Working For God or Government?

"Who do you Pledge Your Allegiance To?"

Bible Verse – *"For we are God's workmanship, created in Christ Jesus to do good works, which God prepared in advance for us to do"* - *Ephesians 2:10 (NIV)*

Have you ever thought about who you are really working for? Are you working now, or have you ever worked for a governmental agency? If so, have you stopped to think how your position relates to the Bible and specifically how it relates to God's purpose for your life? I believe that the answer would be a resounding *"No"* but that's okay. It's natural for man to forget what we were created by God for. Often, people are shocked to discover that God knows anything about them, and least of all, that God has a plan in mind for them. Most people believe that their faith in God is an individual act and one that they can pull out anytime that they need it. I call this the "Genie in the Bible God". Most people treat God as if he was some magic genie that lives in a Bible and whenever things get so difficult that they can't handle it on their own they open their Bible and cry out "Lord, where are you? I need you now more than ever!" On any other occasion they wouldn't bother to give God as much as the time of day. But that is not what God wants from us.

Throughout this study, our goal is to lead you to understand that there exists a Godly purpose waiting on you to fulfill and the only way for you to fulfill this role is to stop and invite Christ into your heart. You are not going to do it simply by being a "good person" or as a "part-time Christian".

First Responders for God

Most people don't like the idea that someone else may have plans for your life. Let's face it, we all like to be in control, and there is no one who likes to be in control more than a cop. I'm sure that you believe like most people, that you alone are responsible for your successes and your failures. However, I am a strong believer that God develops and uses us as His tool wherever, and whenever needed. I guess you could call us a kind of "First Responder for God". I also believe that God gives individuals the heart and desire for a particular occupation. We are all aware that there are some occupations that not just anyone would be good at. For example, school teachers. It takes a special person to teach. The same with doctors, nurses, pastors, firefighters, lawyers, mechanics, and cooks. The list could go on and on. And while many of us may have the desire to do some of these other occupations we are still in the position of a cop. Why do you think that is? There are plenty of other occupations and professions in which we could leave police work and earn a lot more money, have less stress, work normal hours with weekends and holidays off. So, why are we in this profession? I have asked this question to myself as well as to other officers over the years and the answer is the same, "I don't know?" Personally, I believe that it is God who gave us the desire for our chosen occupation.

For a number of years, I worked as a Field Training Officer (FTO) and in the process trained many law enforcement officers. Some of which, I had to make recommendations to pass or fail them. In my best evaluation these individuals could not perform well in the position of a law enforcement officer. Every cop reading this will understand when I say that not just anyone can be police officer. No matter how strong their desire may be. So, the question really becomes why are YOU in this position? Why, did you make it and others did not? In short, I believe that it was because God saw something in you that He believed you could handle as His instrument. Too often we falsely believe that we alone are responsible for obtaining our own jobs, our own career goals, and our own promotions. See if any of these comments sound familiar to you. "Of course I was selected for the job. After all, I do have a college degree." Or, you may have said something like, "I got the promotion because they picked the best candidate for the job." To think things like this is referred to in the Bible as having sinful pride. In the book of Psalm 10:4-6 we are told the following about having sinful pride; *"In his pride the wicked does not seek him; in all his thoughts there is no room for God. His ways are always prosperous; he is haughty and your laws are far from him; he sneers at all his enemies. He says to himself, "Nothing will shake me; I'll always be happy and never have trouble".(NIV)*

Small Group Scripture Reading – Select someone from your group to read 2 Corinthians 3:5; *"It is not that we think we can do anything of lasting value by ourselves. Our only power and success come from God." (NLT)*

The Bible also tells us in 1 Chronicles 29:12; *"Riches and honor come from you alone, for you rule over everything. Power and might are in your hand, and it is at your discretion that people are made great and given strength"* What this verse tells us is that contrary to your own popular belief, neither you (or me), were the sole person responsible for obtaining your job. None of us really want to believe that God could be at work in our lives it is scary to think that someone who you have turned your back on as a friend is actually the one who is silently working to direct you in your daily routine. We don't want to feel obligated to God. However, God saw a potential, a purpose, and a plan in you that He knew only you could handle. Maybe this was something that has already occurred in the past, and you never knew it. Or, it may be some future set of circumstances that is waiting ahead for you to fulfill. So, always thank God for your career, and pray that He may use you to make a difference in the life of someone who may be spiritually hurting.

Trusting God

Over the years, you may have forgotten just how many different jobs that you have applied for in your life that you really wanted more than anything else in the world. Yet somehow you never got past the front door? I sure do. Over the years, I have applied for a number of jobs both in and out of law enforcement that I felt I was qualified for. And in a few cases, I was called back for second and third interview. However, I never got the jobs that I wanted. After much prayer and spending some quite time with God, I began to understand why I was not selected for these jobs. It's simple. God had other plans for me. Looking back on it now, had I been selected for any of those great paying jobs it may have entrenched me even further into something that God didn't want me to do. You see, God has a plan for my life just as he does your life. God wants to use us! Don't deny God the opportunity to use you as one of His first responders by not accepting or choosing to believe in Him. I like what the Bible says in 1st Corinthians 12:6 *(NLT) "There are different ways God works in our lives, but it is the same God who does the work through all of us"*

Small Group Question – *Discuss among your group the following questions.*

- *In what ways do you believe that God can, or will, reveal His purposes and plan for your life?*

- *Do you believe that God has already worked some purpose or plan in your life?*

God Doesn't Have Time for Me

Another reason that we don't always believe that God can be an active participant in our daily lives is our erroneous thoughts of self-pity. We say things like, "God has so much stuff going on that He

Small Group Scripture Reading – Read John 3:16 ; *"For God so loved the world that he gave his only Son, so that everyone who believes in him will not perish but have eternal life".*

doesn't need to be bothered with my insignificant life." You may believe that with all God has on his plate, such as dealing with billions of people on a sinful earth you may say to yourself "Why would God want to waste His time on me?" Simply stated, because, every life and every person matters to God.

It doesn't matter if you consider yourself to be the worst sinner of all time, God still wants you to come to Him and accept Him into your life. Never underestimate the fact that God knows each of us by name and deed. The Bible tells us this in Matthew 10:30, *"And the very hairs on your head are all numbered."* Believe it, we are in a career that we may have accepted, but it is a career that God has selected for us. Otherwise, you would not be in your position as a peace officer. You would be doing some other profession that He wanted you in. After all, God is the guiding light in our lives. In order to properly serve Him by the gifts that He has bestowed upon us, we must watch, listen, and be observant of the events that are happening in the lives of the people with who we encounter.

No Laughing Matter

Give me the number one answer in a police oral board on the question, "Why do you want to be a police officer?" Well, I can tell you what the answer is not. It is not, "Because I enjoy arresting people." It's not "Because I think the uniform is cool to wear." It's not, "Because "I like to run the siren and watch the red and blue lights flash." And rest assured it is not, "Because "I like to shoot people and carry a gun." The number one answer is, "Because I want to help people." This is exactly the same answer that all the seasoned cops laugh at. But it's no laughing matter. God has personally, and very uniquely, hardwired this desire to help others into your being. God has also placed that same desire in those laughing senior cops, who at one time also wanted to "help people." themselves. Really, the only difference between a rookie and a senior cop is that the senior cop has probably forgotten their answer to this same question, and have allowed years of on-the-job cynicism to creep into their lives, all the while pushing God aside.

Small Group Scripture Reading – Read Galatians 6:2; *"Share each other's troubles and problems, and in this way obey the law of Christ"*

It's all termed differently, but it's why soldiers die in battle, because they wanted to serve their country. As a law enforcement officer, you also want to serve your country but you do so by serving your community, which translates to "helping people".

Pastor Rick Warren in his book, 'The Purpose Driven Life' states that *"you were created for a purpose."* The Bible in Psalm 138:8 says; *"The Lord will fulfill, his purpose for me."* Personally, I do not disagree with that statement, and from my own spiritual stand-point, that one verse caused me to re-evaluate my own spiritual life which as a direct result you are now reading this book. Once you begin to think about what gifts that you have been given and how you can start giving back to God through your service to Him. Then, with God on your side there will be no task either to big, or too small for you to conquer.

A Big Responsibility for God

As we already know, being a law enforcement officer is a huge responsibility that is not to be taken lightly. But being a "Christian Cop" is an even greater responsibility. As Christians, we will always be tempted into sin and we will always try to walk the three "P's" which is short for the *"perfect path of perfection."* But God doesn't ask that we be perfect. Besides, I don't know about you? But, I don't want to have to be "perfect". To be perfect makes you the stand-out in a crowd, to be perfect can garner us negative attention. Trying to be the perfect police officer, or the perfect parent, brings stress upon us, our jobs, and our family. At the same time you cannot use the excuse of "not being perfect" as a way to just give in and allow sin to overtake our lives. It also does not mean that our God given purposes and responsibilities have been diminished in some way. God doesn't want perfection He just wants you to accept Him into your life.

Small Group Questions - *Answer the following questions True or False*

As law enforcement officers we are taught never to back down from fear or to retreat from danger posed against us while in the official performance of our duties?

Circle one   True - False

As law enforcement officers we have the full authority of the badge and the office that we hold behind us in order to carry out our lawful duties and responsibilities?

Circle one   True - False

As "Peacekeepers" for Christ, should never back down or retreat from fear or danger posed against us while in our official performances of our duties.

Circle one   True - False

Try to Make a Difference in a Life

The early morning hours of March 12, 2005 was not going to be like any other day for twenty-six year old Ashley Smith, a widowed mother of a five year-old daughter. Ashley was held hostage in her apartment for seven hours by Brian Nichols, an escaped prisoner from an Atlanta courthouse who in his ensuing escape shot and killed a Fulton County Judge, a court reporter, a Deputy Sheriff, and an off-duty US Customs Service Special Agent. During the time that he held Ashley captive she had the opportunity to talk to him about God and read to him from the Bible and a chapter from the book, "The Purpose Driven Life" by Pastor Rick Warren. As Ashley read from Chapter 33 of "The Purpose Driven Life" book, something must have struck this murderer. Because he asked Ashley to, "read it again." No one except Brian Nichols and God know for sure what happened next, but the fact of the matter remains, this killer referred to Ashley Smith as an "angel sent by God" and when he asked Ashley what he should do, she told him "to give your self up to the police." And that is exactly what he did. This escaped prisoner who eluded capture for twenty-six hours and who shot and killed four individuals, and who assaulted at least three other individuals, in the end waved a white shirt and surrendered to the police.

What caused this incident to end the way it did? I personally believe that God had a hand in it. God does work in mysterious ways, and on that fateful day I believe that God worked through this young lady in order to reach out to someone, a sinner, who needed to know the "Good News" of Jesus Christ in an immediate way. However, one thing is certain. Ashley Smith had a choice. She could have sat quietly and cried about her situation. She could have begged and pleaded for her life from this killer for the entire seven hours that she was held captive. Instead, what did she do? She took a leap of faith and stepped outside of her comfort zone and began to speak to this killer as if he was just a fellow sinner. Just as if he was another "lost soul" who was searching for God. Ashley Smith recognized that she needed to rely on her faith and trust in God to allow her to get through a very difficult situation.

Here is the question that I have for every officer reading this. If an ordinary citizen can talk to an escaped killer as if he was simply a "lost soul" what is to prevent us in law enforcement from doing the same thing? What? The government we work for? God created and ordained it. Read Romans 13 if you have forgotten. Why, because we are supposed to remain neutral? That applies to our enforcement of the law, and not our spiritual beliefs.

I believe that we should all take a spiritual lesson from Ashley Smith and learn the following 3 things;

1.   We need to trust that God will never leave our side and works daily in the lives of His people who have accepted Him.

2.   That God will get us through any difficult situation in which we find ourselves in.

3.   Never miss an opportunity to tell someone about the "Good News" of Jesus Christ.

Small Group Discussion – Discuss among your group the following questions.

Do you believe that you would have reacted in the same manner as Ashley Smith?

Do you believe that God can work through people like Ashley Smith to achieve some greater goal or purpose?

To borrow a line from the popular radio talk show host, "Dr. Laura" who always closes her radio show with the following line: "Now go do the right thing," I would challenge each of you as Christian officers, that each day that you go into your communities to "protect and serve" that you "go do the right thing for God" and never forget who you are really working for.

Chapter Nine

Falling Down

"When we become cynical without God on the job"

Bible Verse –"Therefore do not worry about tomorrow for tomorrow can worry about itself; each day has enough trouble of its own." - Matthew 6:34 (NIV)

The title of this session, "Falling Down," was also the title of a popular film from 1993 staring actor Michael Douglas. In this movie, the main character, William Foster, plays a laid-off worker who is employed by a military defense manufacturer. Needless to say, this man does not have a good day. Laid-off from his job and recently separated from his wife and child, he encounters heavy traffic on his way home to give his daughter a birthday gift. He becomes so impatient with the traffic that he leaves his car parked on the freeway and takes off on foot. While walking, he encounters racial and ethnic tensions and more traffic jams. He sees violent acts, armed robberies, and is himself attacked and mugged. Throughout the movie, he becomes so cynical and burdened with the hectic stress of life and with his own personal suffering that he mentally *"snaps"* and becomes a one-man vigilante. He steals a gun, robs a fast-food restaurant, and begins to issue out his own unique brand of street justice to each situation that he encounters. Each scene of the movie is like a branch that is broken away from a tree.

Eventually, at the end of the movie, he has a shoot-out with police and in the ensuing gun battle is killed.

How many of us have become so cynical or jaded at some point in our career, that we have either had, or came close to having a mental breakdown because of the stress associated with our jobs? If the truth be known, too many officers have nearly *"snapped"* and lost it all just like the character in the movie, and I am sure we have know other officers that have lost it all.

Small Group Question - Answer honestly among your small group the following questions.

Write down and discuss with the group the times that you have found yourself being cynical towards people. This can be either on, or off the job.

• _____

• _____

How did you feel afterwards? Did you feel that you could have handled the situation better?

• _____

How do you think that God would want you to handle the situation?

• _____

Cynicism at Work And At Home

This idea of cynicism and of being bitter, seem to be most true for anyone who works with the general public and who can become understandably *"grouchy"* over a period of time. This list could include, policeman, fireman, school teachers, nurses, doctors, store cashiers, waiters or waitresses, mechanics, the list can go on and on. We in law enforcement know what it is to be asked the same questions day after day with no variety. Pretty soon, the answers we give become like an overly-rehearsed tune, where there is no real conversation to it, but instead more of an unenthusiastic muttering of details.

During my own law enforcement career, I found it to be true that as people asked their questions, I had already figured out where their line of questioning was going. I kept my answers brief to get through them quickly and onto something that I haven't been quizzed on a million times before. But silently, under my breath, I would think to myself, "its little wonder you are in the situation you are, because you are asking such a stupid question!" So, I would give each citizen two answers. The verbal polite answer and then I would give them the other silent, "real answer" under my breath. Over the years, this built-up cynicism caused me personal stress everywhere I went, both in my personal and professional life. Trips to the grocery store, filling up at the gas station, going out to eat, you name it.

Like most of us in the profession of law enforcement, I became suspicious of everything and everybody. I would begin to judge and criticize anyone that I would see. For example if I saw a bearded and tattooed man standing in front of me, I would think to myself, "I wonder how many times he has been in jail?" Usually, I was right. But, after a while, I felt as if I had become the character "Radar" from popular 1970's television series M*A*S*H. If you remember, Radar always had it in the hand before anyone could ask for it. This issue of cynicism took me years to overcome and it had a negative effect in both my personal life and in my relationship with God.

The Reason for Our Cynicism...

A major factor behind most of our stress could be that we are to busy living a life of being cynical without allowing God to share in our lives. Whenever we find ourselves in this position of being cynical or, having a jaded attitude about our jobs, or with the people whom we encounter, we should remember that our cynicism is not of God's doing, but rather that of Satan. The Bible tells us in James 1:16-17, *"So don't be misled....whatever is good and perfect comes to us from God."* Satan would like for us to focus on our own self-issues and the negativity found in both our lives and our jobs. For whenever we do that, our minds are not focusing on God but rather on ourselves. This robs us of our desire to turn all our problems over to God.

Small Group Scripture Reading - Read together as a small group, the following Bible verses;

• *"It's smart to be patient, but it's stupid to lose your temper" - Proverbs 14:29*

• *"But when the Holy Spirit controls our lives he will produce this kind of fruit in us; love, joy, peace, patience " - Galatians 5:22*

• *" And he passed in front of Moses, proclaiming, "The Lord, the Lord, the compassionate and gracious God, slow to anger, abounding in love and faithfulness" - Exodus 34:6*

• *"An angry person stirs up a fight, and a hothead does much wrong" - Proverbs 29:22*

Turning our Problems over to God

Often times, we fail to understand that our cynicism, worry, stress, and anger come from us trying to handle our own problems instead of turning them over to God. In my own life it has been my experience that when I start to think that I know it all, and just when I believe that I have it all figured out, it is then I began to realize just how much I didn't really know. I believe part of our problem is that as law enforcement officers we are taught to handle situations on our own. After all, aren't we paid to make life-or-death decisions in a split second? While we are in the official performance of our duties this may be acceptable, but it is not acceptable to try and handle things on your own in matters where it comes to your personal, family or spiritual life.

Small Group Scripture Reading – Read the following Bible verse among your group. Proverbs 3:5-6; *"Trust in the Lord with all you're your heart and lean not on your own understanding. In all ways acknowledge Him and He will make your path straight".*

This attitude of going it alone is often referred to as "spiritual immaturity." It is important for us to understand that God never intended for us to be a "Lone Ranger" Christian. It has always been His desire to see us connected to the body of Christ, which is the Church. Being connected to a Church and its members gives us a firm spiritual foundation for us to rest all of our problems and

---

Small Group Scripture Reading – Read the following Bible verse as found in Hebrews 10:25; *"Let us not give up meeting together, as some are in the habit of doing, but let us encourage one another-and all the more as you see the Day approaching"*

---

concerns on. God knew this and is the reason why the Bible repeatedly makes reference to us being part of a Church family.

If, for whatever reason, you can't bring yourself to be a part of a Church family at this time, at the very least surround yourself with Christian law enforcement officers. Attend a PeaceKeepers Bible study. Use this study as an opportunity to build up your spiritual maturity. Take the time to visit a variety of churches until you find one that you would enjoy returning to every Sunday

God and Superman?

Did you find that the stress encountered by the character in the film "Falling Down", sounds a lot like what law enforcement officers see on a daily basis? Don't we as law enforcement officers see man's inhumanity towards one another, stresses of driving Code 3 in traffic jams, racial and ethnic tensions, violence and homicide, child abuse, sexual battery, alcoholism, drug abuse, domestic violence, robbery and thievery? It makes one wonder what God must have been thinking when He blessed the position of a law enforcement officer? Personally, I believe that God had to be thinking about "Superman" when he blessed the position of peace officers. In fact, I'm positive that is what God was thinking. I mean, what other profession can see the troubles of life so vividly and be there at the exact time in order to make a life changing difference?

Read aloud the following Bible verse, Romans 13, verse 4 - *"For he is God's servant to do you good."* Anyone who is God's servant and is given authority to do good works will possess a certain amount of Godly strength and character. However, our free will as humans sometimes gets in the way of our Godly tasks. As peace officers we can easily forget about our purpose in serving God, and instead become distracted with our own problems. When this happens, our spiritual strength can come under attack by Satan and in turn he (not God) will magnifies all of our problems so that they seem so difficult that we can't climb out of them. The Bible tells us very vividly that this is a game that Satan can play with our life. It is found in 1 Peter 5:8; *"Be careful, watch out for attacks from Satan, your great enemy. He prowls around like a hungry, roaring lion, looking for some victim to tear apart."*

Had our character in the movie *Falling Down*, tried some of these tips and turned his life over to Christ instead of allowing his emotions to overtake him, in what way would the movie have turned out differently? I can sum that up. There would have been no movie at all. There is a lesson here for all of us. Whenever our emotions get the best of us, we need to turn to God. We should never forget that with Christ's ever-loving patience in our hearts there is no drama, no anger, and no stress that both you and He can not handle together. Seem hard to believe? Just give Christ a chance. Accept Him into your life today. Allow God to intervene on your behalf and allow the personal peace and joy that only a life with Christ can give you enter into your life.

Small Group Discussion - After reading the above statement, answer the following questions in a group setting.

- *What is your personal stress, cynicism, worry, or anger that impacts your life?*

- *How can you better release this stress, cynicism, worry, or anger?*

Over the next couple of weeks, I would challenge each one of you to establish your own "cynicism" work plan. Ask yourself the question, how can I personally remove the anger, worry and stress, in my life that will prevent me from Falling down without Christ in my life? Additionally, I would like to encourage each member of your small group to write down and read each of the following five Bible verses, one for each day of work week (Monday through Friday). Cut them out; carry them with you in your patrol vehicle, briefcase, locker, or duty bag. Commit each one to memory and when things become difficult reach for one of these Bible verses!

- *"Rejoice in the Lord always. I will say it again, Rejoice! Let your gentleness be evident to all that the Lord is near. Do not be anxious about anything"* – Philippians 4: 4-6

- *"Unload all your worries on Him since he is looking after you"* - 1 Peter 5:7

- *"Hot tempers cause arguments"* - Proverbs 14:29

- *" And don't sin by letting anger gain control over you"* - Ephesians 4:26

- *"For I am the Lord, your God, who takes hold of your right hand and says to you, do not fear; I will help you."* - Isaiah 41:13

***Some Facts about Worry and Stress** By Thomas S. Kepler (1898–1963)*

40 % of your worries never happen

30% of your worries concern the past

12% of your worries are needless health concerns

10% of your worries are insignificant and petty issues

8% of your worries are actual, legitimate concerns

Chapter Ten

Is There a Life Beyond the Badge?

"What to do when we leave a career in law enforcement"

Bible Verse- *"God has given each of you some special abilities; be sure to use them to help each other. Passing on to other's God's many kinds of blessings." - 1 Peter 4:10*

Have you ever stopped to think what it will be like once you leave a career in law enforcement? Maybe, you have recently retired or resigned from a position in law enforcement and you are not really sure what to do with your life? After twenty years or more of serving your community, you have now retired and are no longer serving or protecting. Maybe, you were injured on the job and had to take early medical retirement. So, you may be asking the logical question "What should I do with my life now"? For many officers, retirement can be a scary time in their lives. Possibly, for the first time in your life you are stepping out into a new and different world where, for only the second time in the last twenty years or more, you are now going outside the safety and security of the uniform and the badge. There are no more fellow officers there "backing you up." Walking into the same police station where you once roamed freely, you are now questioned by some rookie officer behind the desk, given a visitor's pass, and escorted around. You are treated slightly better than the *'crooks'* that you once escorted through the same building only months earlier. Few remember your accomplishments, and even fewer remember you. What a shock this can be!

Injured on the Job

An even bigger shock is the number of our fellow law enforcement officers who have been permanently injured as a result of an on-duty police action. While we do honor, and should honor, those officers who have died in the line of duty, we barely, if at all, remember the number of officers who are paralyzed in wheelchairs with bullets lodged in their spine, and those that were seriously injured in pursuits and traffic accidents. And there are plenty more with facial, body, or hand deformities. How many of us remember these heroes? I believe that we purposely don't want to visit or associate with these injured officers because it reminds us to much of our own mortality. But this is not what Jesus would do. Remember, throughout the Bible there are numerous examples of how Jesus helped those that needed it most. He approached, healed, and ministered to those that would otherwise be considered society's outcast. This is where every cop reading this book could be the living example of Jesus Christ. How many officers could fulfill a Godly purpose for their lives by simply ministering to injured officers? By visiting, praying with, or helping the family of the officer to get over these difficult times may be the reason you were placed into your job. Yet, when it comes to those officers who have been seriously injured we often have the unintentional tendency to treat them as if they were law enforcement outcasts.

Although injured and medically retired, the officer still needs to understand that there exists for them a Godly plan. It may be to help rookie cops learn how to avoid being in the placed into the same situation as they were. It may be as a way to show other Christian officers that they can still maintain a strong faith in God despite their injuries. It may be to start-up an organization to help raise funds for injured officers and their families. No matter the situation we find ourselves in, we still have a purpose and a call to service on God's behalf. Remember, we serve God by serving others. And if we in law enforcement can't show Christian love towards our fellow injured and crippled officers, how can we ever make a difference in the lives of ordinary citizens that need our help?

Small Group Scripture Reading – Read the following two different Bible verses;

- 1 Corinthians 12:4-7; *"There are different kinds of gifts, but the same Spirit. There are different kinds of service, but the same Lord. There are different kinds of working, but the same God works all of them in all men. Now to each one the manifestation of the Spirit is given for the common good"*

- 1 Peter 4:10-11- *"Each one should use whatever gift he has received to serve others, faithfully administering God's grace in its various forms. If anyone speaks, he should do it as one speaking the very words of God. If anyone serves, he should do it with the strength God provides, so that in all things God may be praised through Jesus Christ. To him be the glory and the power for ever and ever"*

Throughout this study we have learned that it is not by chance that we are all called by God to do this difficult line of work. We have learned that the Lord created each of us for a particular purpose and that he has endowed each of us with skills necessary to accomplish the job of a "PeaceKeeper for Christ." So, what does the Bible have to say about those of us who leave our chosen careers? Are we going against what God has ordained for us? The short answer is "No." In fact, each of us has been provided by God with our very own set of knowledge, skills, and abilities that He wants us to use as a way to serve others with. In this chapter, we will take a closer look at just what knowledge, skills, and abilities that God has provided each of us with skills in which we should use not only as an "income maker," but as a "glory maker" for God's benefit.

The Bible and Retirement

Sadly, many police officers feel that once they retire they have nothing else to give. They have given freely of themselves throughout their entire career to the communities that they so honorably served, and since they have now retired many feel as if they have lost their purpose to their life. In the entire Bible, there is only one verse where it refers to the word retirement. Naturally, in Biblical days there was no such thing as retirement, 401K accounts, social security, union wages, direct deposits, or long-term health benefits. In fact, the only reference to retirement is found in Numbers 8, verses 24-26 when God directed Moses to address the Levites who were building the temple. Specifically verse 25 states the following; *"but at the age of fifty, they must retire from their regular service and work no longer."* But in verse 26, God tells Moses, *"They may assist their brothers in performing their duties at the Tent of Meeting, but they themselves must not do the work."*

There is no further explanation in the Bible, nor is there any other reference as to why God did not want men over fifty years of age to work. However, if you noticed God stills directs them to assist in the building, just not physically work, meaning that they still have value too their life.

Your Knowledge, Skills, and Abilities

In the Federal government when you apply for a job, one of the requirements in addition to a job application is something called "KSA's", which stands for *"Knowledge, Skills, and Abilities"*. In order to qualify for a job, you must write out all of your *"knowledge, skills, and abilities"* that make you qualified for a particular position. But did you know that we already have our KSA's written out by God and that He has given them to each of us as a gift? God knows each one of our KSA's and he has perfectly placed them into our being. While these skills can be numerous most of them we use on a regular basis in police work. In the past, we have referred to these skills as *"street sense," "mother's intuition,"*

Small Group Scripture Reading – Read the following Bible verses.

- 1 Corinthians 12:6 *"God works through different people in different ways, but it is the same God who achieves his purpose through them all"*

- Ephesians 2:10 – "For we are God's *workmanship, created in Christ Jesus to do good works which God prepared in advance for us to do"*

"street smarts," "police wise," and the list goes on. But have you have ever stopped to wonder where these skills came from and why God gave them to you specifically? The truth of the matter is that most of us have never stopped to think about it. We just assumed that we developed and honed these skills all by our selves. Just think, all of the skills that once made you a great cop were given to you as a gift by God to help guide you to a point in your life where you may be able to serve others with the gifts, skills, and abilities given by Him.

Small Group Exercise – Read and answer the following questions as a group. *Read Romans 12 verse 6-8 – then discuss among the group your thoughts on this verse.*

What natural or God given types of KSA's do you believe that God has blessed you with? Write below some examples. Some examples may be the following; patience, leadership, etc.

- _____

- _____

- _____

Small Group Exercise - Let's take a brief review of your God given KSA's and see how you can use them for God's benefit. On a scale of 1 to 5, with 5 being the best and 1 being the least. Rate the skills that you have

- _____ - *ability to communicate (orally or in writing)*

- _____ - *physical fitness*

- _____ - *administrative abilities*

- _____ - *artistic skills (i.e.) writing, producing, drawing,*

- _____ - *knowledge of the Bible, religious studies*

- _____ - *desire to serve*

- _____ - *compassion for your fellow man*

- _____ - *ability to listen*

- _____ - *teaching / instructing*

- _____ - *leadership ability*

- _____ - *patience with people.*

> ***Small Group Exercise*** - Read the following Bible verse found in Luke 9:23; *"Then Jesus said to all the people, if any of you want to be my followers, you must forget about yourself. You must take up your cross each day and follow me."*

Small Group Exercise - Fill in the blank. The answers can be located at the end of this chapter.

1.   Become an 'active' church member - don't just come to church on Sunday ONLY to 'ride the oak' (sitting on the pew). Become involved in feeding the souls of _____

2.   Begin to lead a life of _____ - remember life is not about "SERVE US" but rather SERVICE. To freely give something back for a much bigger cause.

3.   Have the courage to forget about _____ in order to honor Christ and meet another person's needs.

4.   Get   connected   to   a   _____
Community.

5.   _____ For God's guidance in the life and in the lives of others.

List and name some other areas where you can assist your church, community, or fellow man while also leading them productively to a life with Christ?

- _____

- _____

- _____

- _____

Giving Back in Service to God

Retirement from, or leaving, a career in law enforcement does not mean that you will no longer have to *"protect and serve"* your fellow man, but instead it means that you will turn to a new page in your service to God. Much like a person who is blind or deaf can utilize their other senses of the brain you are no different. As you know, these people turn their sensory perception, which the majority of us take for granted into a much stronger skill. So, leaving a career in law enforcement is no different. You simply turn those same God-given KSA's that you used all these years to keep you safe and make you an outstanding cop into a much stronger skill that can be utilized to serve God's Kingdom and to lead others to Christ. After all, it was God that gave you the skills, so why not give something back to Him in return for blessing you? "But how can I do this?" you ask. It is simple. First, discover what you enjoy doing best, and then use it for God's glory.

A great illustration of this is the following example. In one of our PeaceKeepers chapters there was a retired officer who had a real talent for hiking the mountains and canyons of southern

California. When he retired, he was offered various jobs as a hiking guide, all of which he turned down. Instead, he chose to lead a group of Church young people on hikes where he pointed out God's creations and stopped for "Bible breaks" along the trails. This is a great example of giving back to God through your gifts and talents. So, to answer our small group title, "Is there a life beyond the badge?" The answer is a strong "YES."

No matter why you leave a career in law enforcement or whatever you decide do after retirement always remember to do it for the glory of God. If I were to give one piece of advice to anyone reading this study it would be this. No matter what occupation you are in, go discover your purpose for serving God and then live it out to the fullest. Don't waste your time setting on the sidelines of life thinking about what you might do, instead pray about it, and follow your heart and go do it! God wants "doers". He wants "men and women of action". The Bible in James 1:22-25 confirms this in the following way. *"Do not merely listen to the word, and so deceive yourselves. Do what it says. Anyone who listens to the word but does not do what it says is like a man who looks at his face in a mirror and, after looking at himself, goes away and immediately forgets what he looks like. But the man who looks intently into the perfect law that gives freedom, and continues to do this, not forgetting what he has heard, but doing it— he will be blessed in what he does.*

ANSWER KEY FOR
IS THERE LIFE BEYOND THE BADGE?

1. feeding the souls of **OTHERS**

2. begin to lead a life of **SERVICE**

3. courage to forget about **MYSELF**

4. get connected to a **SMALL GROUP** community

5. **PRAY** for God's guidance

Chapter Eleven

"10-8" In-Service With Christ

"When We Allow Our Career to Define Our Christian Life"

Bible Verse – *"Whatever you do, do your work heartily, as for the Lord rather than for men; knowing that from the Lord you will receive the reward of the inheritance. It the Lord Christ whom you serve"* - *Colossians 3:23-24*

Career choices are important by the world's standards because they largely determine your income, standard of living, community status, how both your co-workers and family view you. But did you also know that your personal life is defined by your career? Family and friends evaluate your general satisfaction with life; your self-esteem, emotional well-being, and the use of your time based upon your job. For example, how many times have we heard, "Well, the job has him down." Or, "She worked hard all weekend and just couldn't make it to church today" or, "I would love to go, but I have to work."

Even before sin entered the human race God instituted work. The Bible tells us in Genesis 2:15 the following; *"The Lord God took the man and put him into the Garden of Eden to cultivate it and keep it."* The very first thing that the Lord did with Adam was to put him to work. We don't have to look far in today's society to see why we work, and why our careers define so much of our life. Simply stated because there is so much material "stuff" out in the world that we desire we attempt to maintain a style of living that is hard to achieve. We are like a mouse, caught in a maze and can never reach the cheese. But have you stopped to think that God may not want us to work hard for the material things of life? But why, you ask? "Doesn't God, want me to "support" my family and "provide for them"? The answer is "yes", He does. However, God does not want us so weighted down with debt from the material things of life that we become enslaved to our jobs in order to pay for them.

In those cases, our jobs can take us away from Christ and our service back to Him. The same could be said about our careers. The question that we all need to ask ourselves is the following;

Small Group Question - Feel free to answer this question among your group. Write your answers below and answer honestly.

Why do have a career and why do we work?

- _____

- _____

- _____

List here a few of the material "wants" that you have 'worked' to achieve. Include those that you are 'working' to obtain as well. Some examples may be a home, a new car, a computer, or something else.

- _____

- _____

- _____

Gifts to God

I realize that having to give anything back can be difficult, much less, finding out that you should be giving back to God. But what am I supposed to give back you ask? "What can I give to God? After all He is so BIG, and I am so small". While it sounds difficult, it is actually very easy. God only wants three things from you. I call these your **"Gifts to God"**.

1. *God wants you to turn your life over to Him*, and accept Jesus Christ as your personal savior.

2. *God wants you to give back to Him*, though your talents, your worship, and through your service to the Him

3. *God wants you to lead others* to come to know Him just as you do.

These three gifts are important, because together they lay the foundation needed for your spiritual life. Talk with your Minister, Pastor, your agency Chaplain, or your church leader for information on how to turn your life over to God. Also, at the end of this chapter we will tell you in detail how you may go about turning your life over to Christ today. Remember, you are never too old to accept Jesus Christ into your life.

The second point is living a life of service for Christ. This is what I call "giving back" to God. Our law enforcement work is only half of it. Did you know that the Bible directs us in Galatians 5:13 (NIV) to *"serve one another in love."* As a law enforcement officer there is a number of ways that you can do this for example, by spending time to talk with a grieving crime victim, by enforcing the law fairly and without prejudice, by not viewing citizens as a *"stat"* but instead as people who need to be corrected and finally, by viewing the community that you police as the spiritually lost. In doing this, I believe that God will allow you to be "His instrument" to make a spiritual impact in the life of someone that you encounter.

Small Group Exercise - Take a moment and place the following topics by number in the area of importance for you. You do not need to share your answers with the group.

Topics	*Order of Importance*
▪ Family	1 -
▪ God	2 –
▪ Work	3 –
▪ Time Alone	4 -

Cops and Gangs

Let's be honest. Many officers have developed an association with their law enforcement jobs that is really no different than the criminal gangs that we chase after. For example, ask any gang banger the question, "Why do you belong to a gang?" and they will tell you, "Because they accept me" or, "I have a sense of belonging," or, they may tell you "I identify with the gang like a family." I believe that many law enforcement officers have found this same sense of belonging within their jobs, their shift partners, or in their department. In those cases, the individual officer has found a "sense of acceptance" within their job. Once we get into this mode of being accepted by other cops, the fact of the matter is, nothing else-matters. This includes our family, our spouse, dating, church, or God. Unfortunately, having this attitude "love of work" accounts for many of the law enforcement divorces. Now, to be fair, it is not only law enforcement that can be guilty of this sense of belonging to the job.

Anyone, in any profession, can have this same preoccupation with work. The problem lies not in our choice of careers, but in placing your career before everything else including God. If you have a preoccupation with your job, and see your job becoming your life, ask God to show you how to free yourself from these chains, and learn to stop living for the job, and start living for God through your job.

Small Group Bible Verse Reading – Read the following Bible verse as found in *Exodus 20:3* - *"You shall have no other gods before me."*

Small Group Discussion - Answer and discuss among the group

- *Do we in law enforcement identify with ourselves and the agencies that we work for in the same way as gang members do. If so, why do you believe this is?*

- *Simply because we can "relate" to one another as police officers does that mean we can not relate to one another as "Christian Cops"?*

- *Can our jobs be a "god" as described in Exodus 20:3?*

A Leap of Faith

Many years ago, I left a great career with a Sheriff's Department in Florida in order to pursue a new career within federal law enforcement. While the majority of my Sheriff's Department co-workers supported me in leaving, there were more than a few who had felt that I had *"abandoned the team."* They felt hurt or jealous that I had left the agency. In short, I was snubbed, except for the closest of my friends. But something inside of me said that this would be a good move for both my wife and I. Although my wife was not as sure about the move as I was. My wife had become extremely content with her job, her home, and living near both of our families. She was in her "comfort zone". Ultimately, she agreed and made the move across the country to Southern California based upon a one year trial. The first few months we were living in Los Angeles she hated it. Nothing seemed to be going right. She changed jobs twice. The apartment that we were in raised the rent unexpectedly. Things were going so poorly that I thought that our one year trial would turn into a three month nightmare. But eventually, we found a home in the suburbs and settled in. We now belong to a great Church and a terrific Church family.

What I learned from this move, is that strengthening our spiritual life is a lot like moving. Sometimes we need to step outside of our comfort zones in order to make the biggest impact possible for God. While at first it may seem scary, sometimes you have to take a "leap of faith" in order to reap the benefits of knowing the joy that can be found in serving the Lord.

God needs people who are not afraid to step outside of their comfort zones in order to accomplish the plans that He has set for us. Don't be afraid *to "step out on faith"* and follow a life with God. We are given a clear command as found in the book of Matthew 10:38-39 to step out on faith by telling us to take up your cross and follow a life with Christ. Read the following verse; *"and anyone who does not take his cross and follow me is not worthy of me. Whoever finds his life will lose it and whoever loses his life for my sake will find it.* If you have never accepted Christ into your heart, do so now. Take up your cross and follow Him. He will never let you fail!

The Perfect Job

During my law enforcement career, I have known people myself included, who in the process of working, spent so much time making and molding their career into "the perfect job" that their career begins to define and shape their life? Nothing else mattered except making the way to the top. Traditionally, we as employees are taught that the harder we work within our jobs, then the higher we will move up the career ladder. Have you ever been told by your boss that you are up for the next promotion? What happens? You work harder than ever for a short period of time just to prove that you have what it takes to be the company player. Then you are slapped back into reality when the "rookie" gets the promotion over you. What happened you ask? The answer is that you put your faith and trust in someone other than God. You didn't take the time to see if your promotion was part of God's plan.

We sometimes forget that God doesn't need just Chief's in his army but he needs foot soldiers as well. Instead of seeking the "perfect job" based upon a higher salary, more prestige, a great sign-on bonus, or any other material benefits maybe you should take a look at perfect job that God has already given you. Maybe, you need to learn to serve God in your present job and then He can bless you in some other way for your faithfulness to Him.. The Bible tells us in the book of Psalm 75:6-7 the following; *"for promotion and power come from nowhere on earth, but only from God."*

Develop today your plan for being faithful to God as part of your service back to Him. Become a foot solider for God today!

Small Group Exercise - Read the following Bible verse together and then answer the questions; - Psalm 75:6-7; *"For promotion and power come from nowhere on earth, but only from God." (LBT)*

- What does this verse mean to you? Discuss among your group your answers.

- Have you been guilty of making your job into the "perfect career?"

Where Is God In Our Work?

As we have discovered. It is not your boss or you, for that matter which controls whether or not you will be promoted, but rather it is all based upon God's timing and plan for our lives. It's a sad fact of life that our culture leaves God out of work. In today's modern work ethic, employees are taught to believe that they alone control their career successes and promotions. As a result, people are unknowingly allowing their career choices to define their life instead of allowing Christ to lead their lives. How many families and marriages have been destroyed by this way of thinking? How many lives have been non-committed to living a life without Christ? Sadly, the answer is too many. Do not merely look out for your own personal interests, but also for the interests of others. How many of us can actually say we subscribe to what the Bible tells us in Philippians 4:11-13; *"I am not saying this because I am in need, for I have learned to be content whatever the circumstances. I know what it is to be in need, and I know what it is to have plenty. I have learned the secret of being content in any and every situation, whether well fed or hungry, whether living in plenty or in want. I can do everything through him who gives me strength"*.

When you can sincerely pray this prayer, then your job will no longer be the focus of everything that is in your life. Try to be content with your jobs and with what the Lord has blessed us with already. Please don't push ahead throwing God, your Church family, and your personal family aside for everything that the world has to offer. Mark 8:36 tells us this; *"What good is it for a man to gain the whole world, yet forfeit his soul?*

Stress at work

If you were to ask your fellow officers around the world what is the number one source of their daily stress that they experience while at work, I am willing to bet that they will say "the management." Funny, it's not the pursuits, it's not the fights, it's not the police work itself, it's not even the many confrontations with the public, it's the management. So, why is it that we try to impress these same people that we don't even want to be around? In short, it's because we don't understand God's part for our work. Let's think here for a moment just what is God's part in our careers?

Small Group Question – Answer among your group the following questions. Be honest in your answer.

True or False - God gives us skills and controls our successes and promotions.

Work must be balanced

Your career however, must be balanced by the other priorities in your life. It is when your career begins to interfere with your relationship with Christ, and with that of your family then it has become the stumbling block in your life. Until this block is removed by turning your life over to Christ, you will not find the "peace and joy" that you have been searching for.

Chapter Twelve

Becoming PeaceKeepers In the Workplace

"When Bosses Go Wild without Christ in their Lives"

Bible Verse – *"Whoever wishes to become great among you shall be your servant"* – Matthew 20:26

Does your boss resemble *"Dr. Evil"*? Have you ever called your supervisor a *"Little Napoleon"* behind his back? I think that we can all agree that the job of a law enforcement officer is stressful enough without having to deal with difficult supervisors and managers. While any organization can have difficult bosses, it seems that law enforcement has more of their fair share of them than most other professions. One explanation for this could be that in police work we see so much negativity in our jobs that it can began to rub off onto those individual officers at an early stage in their career,. Whether it is intentional or not, these *"career hardened"* officers are promoted up through the ranks, thus passing on their negative police attitude along the way in the form of management techniques. In this chapter we will learn some tools that the Christian officer can use to get over these "humps" and to make your workplace a little more Christ-like.

In reality, there are as many different types of managers and supervisors, as there are different types of personalities. The majority of us will always be in subjection to some leader at some point in our career, but the personality type of the boss that we work for really is not the main issue. So what is the main issue, you ask?

It is learning to be a living example of Jesus Christ in our workplaces. Or, you could say that we are learning to be "PeaceKeepers for Christ".

Some Facts on PeaceKeeper's - Fill in the Blanks. The answers can be found at the end of this chapter.

1.PeaceKeepers take the _____

2.PeaceKeepers _____with others.

3.PeaceKeepers focus on the _____, not the person.

4.PeaceKeepers are _____ and willing to compromise.

Small Group Scripture Verse - *"Do everything possible on your part to live in peace with everybody"* - Romans 12:18

Throughout the "PeaceKeepers" small group study, we have attempted to prepare you to be a witness for Christ through your service as a law enforcement officer. But if the fact be told, you really can not serve someone if you don't know them, or fully understand them. Just like a cop needs to know the community that he or she polices, you need to understand your boss. However, the reality is that most of us don't want to get close enough to our bosses in order to understand them or try to make a difference in their leadership.

As most of you know already, cops can be some of the most apathetic individuals. As cops, we wouldn't open our mouths for anything that we see wrong, but we don't mind remaining at a distance and complaining about something we don't like to every person we see. The Bible is our guide for living out our lives as Christians. In the book of 1st Timothy 5:13 we are told; *"Besides, they get into the habit of being idle and going about from house to house. And not only do they become idlers, but also gossips and busybodies, saying things they ought not to."*

A Life of Leisure

It is important for us to understand that as Christians, God doesn't promise us a life of leisure. We are to work for Him while on earth leading others to Christ, striving to lead a life as free from sin as possible, and giving back to God through our service and not through a *"serve us"* attitude . Have you stopped to think that God did not send His Son Jesus to die on the cross to save us, then leave us on some perfect "Christian-filled" earth to sit back and simply enjoy each other's "Godly" company for the rest of eternity. You see, God gives us all a purpose in our trials and difficulties. Often whenever this occurs God is trying to educate us. Personally, I can think of no better training ground than when we are given difficult people to work with.

Once, my Pastor Mike Cobb made a statement during a Sunday service that really stuck out in my mind. I had been struggling with God for sometime over why I kept being assigned to what seemed like the "worst of the worst" supervisors. You know the type 'it's my way or the highway' boss. It seemed that I was all alone in my thinking and in my management techniques. Nothing, meaningful was occurring between myself, who was the first line supervisor and my upper level bosses. Then Pastor Mike, while teaching a lesson in how God uses problems to get our attention, he said the following;

"its okay it you don't get it the first time. God will just keep sending you back to re-take the course." It was the answer I had been searching for. Until I learned to relate to my bosses in such a way that Christ would want me to handle them, He would just keep on giving me bosses that I would continue struggling with. Since that day, I have changed the way that I approach my bosses with problems, and in the way that I interact with them, and it has dramatically reduced my work stress. It's never easy to be a Christian in the workplace especially, a law enforcement workplace.

We should never loose sight of our main goal. That is to share the good news of God's love with those who don't know about Him. As Christians, that is our main purpose in life. To spread God's Good News to the entire world. However, we can't do that without getting close to those who need to know Him the most, and often that can be people who we deal with everyday like supervisors and bosses.

> ***Small Group Bible Reading*** – Read the following Bible passage from Hebrews 12:7 (Msg) *"God is educating you; that's why you must never drop out. He's treating you as dear children. This trouble you're in isn't punishment; it's training."*

Small Group Discussion Questions - Answer and discuss as a group the following questions.

- Would you allow yourself to get close to a difficult boss in order to show them Christ's love?

- Can you view difficult supervisors as someone that may need to hear the "Good News" of Jesus Christ?

An Unwanted Task

While this task of getting close to difficult bosses can seem unwanted, no one ever said that becoming a Christian would be easy. We need to remember that God never wastes a hurt. He has placed you in difficult circumstances to fulfill a role that he has for you at just the right moment in someone else's life. We should look at our "difficult" supervisors and co-workers in the way that Christ would expect us to do, as a work in progress. We should also view them as spiritually lost individuals, and not simply as subordinates to supervisors. We need to see them from the inside-out as a person who needs to know Christ, and may be spiritually hurting themselves. Furthermore, you must show them Christian love without judging them, or losing your own focus on God. This is no small task and it requires a lot of praying and patience on your part. There may be difficult times in your career when your co-workers or even a supervisor may try to sabotage your reputation or try to get a promotion ahead of you. They may even go so far as to try and have you terminated from your job. It is during these times, that we should remember the story of Daniel and the lions den. This story is found in the Bible in Daniel 6 1-28.

Just to recap the story for you; the people under Daniels charge tried to murder Daniel because he refused to worship King Darius. But, even when he was tossed into the lions den Daniel still had respect, (not worship) for the king. Daniel 6:21 tells us that Daniel said the following; *"And Daniel spoke to the king, O'king live forever!"* Daniel knew something that many of us do not. In 1st Peter 2:18 which reads, *"Servants* (employees) *be submissive to your masters* (employers) *with all respect, not only to those who are good and gentle, but also to those who are unreasonable."*

Daniel in a major way took a leap of faith and stepped outside of his comfort zone to tell others, in particular King Darius, about

God. In Daniel 6:26, King Darius is speaking about Daniel's God. He said, *"I make a decree that in all the dominion of my kingdom men are to fear and tremble before the God of Daniel; for he is the living God, and enduring forever, and His kingdom, is one which will not be destroyed, and His dominion will be forever."*

King Darius never would have been able to say this about Daniel's God, which is the one true God, unless two things had not taken place. First, had the Lord not intervened and closed the lion's jaws. Second, if Daniel had not told the king Darius about God's love. You possess the same opportunity as Daniel did to influence not only the people whom you encounter in your police beat, but to influence your supervisors as well.

Special Project for God

God puts us in difficult situations to work with difficult people, as a way to fulfill a need that He has for us at an exact moment in time. Do you believe that God had a purpose for Daniel? I sure do! But, I also believe that God has a plan for us as law enforcement officers as well. Whenever our job tasks become so unbearable and we feel like giving up, we need to remember it is not for our glory, but rather for God's glory!

Recently, I heard a story of a police officer who stopped a man for speeding. He was clocked at doing 76 mph in a 45 mph zone on a dangerous and curvy mountain road. A few weeks after issuing this man a ticket, the Chief called the police officer into his office to show him a letter that the man wrote. The man wrote that the night that the officer stopped him for speeding the man was actually contemplating suicide. He was speeding in order to see how fast he could drive off the mountain road. But after the officer stopped him, it gave him the time to pause and think about what he was doing. He actually drove home and decided not to commit suicide. It was not some random chance that this happened, but it was God always at work, which placed the officer and this man together so that their paths would cross. It was a mission that God needed accomplished and this officer was the instrument. None of us would dispute the idea that God could put us at an exact moment in time as a way to help Him out in that situation. Then why is it so difficult to think that God may have put us with difficult supervisors as a way to help them out, or to show them our Christian spirit, and as a result maybe lead them to Christ?

Small Group Exercise - In one column write the name of some difficult bosses that you have had to deal with. In the other column write the name of your "best" bosses that you have had. Think to yourself about the qualities that each possessed. Find something positive about each one.

Difficult Bosses	Best Bosses

Small Group Question – Answer the following question as a group.

"How do you think that Christ would want you to handle difficult bosses?"

SMALL GROUP TIPS

Here are some tips to assist you in properly dealing with your boss from a Christian stand-point.

- *Don't ever forget that you are a sinner (and sometimes the biggest one of all). This will help you stay grounded and help to keep you from a judgmental attitude.*

- *We lead people to Christ, not by reaching down to them, but instead as one thirsty person bringing water to another.*

- *A Godly person avoids office politics and manipulations*

Angels on the Train

Once, while riding on a commuter train, I was seated next to a young married couple who, like me, noticed a very "Goth" looking person board the train and sit down near us. Obviously shocked by this person's appearance, the husband whispered to his spouse (knowing the spouse and her faults) and said, *"Now, Honey, quit judging and assessing."* For a moment, I thought that God himself had set down next to me. Why? Because I was doing the exact same thing. I was judging and assessing this individual. One of the hardest things for a law enforcement officer to suppress and not do is the very thing that we are paid to do, and that is to judge and assess others. Frankly, our life, and that of our partner may depend on it.

As each of us know, there are countless stories of police officers, when approaching a vehicle on a traffic stop, or approaching a suspect just *"got a funny feeling"* about the situation, and decided to change up their approach, stance, or place their hand on their weapon just in the nick of time. So, telling a cop not to judge and assess people can be as difficult as telling a bird not to sing, or a dog not to bark, or a lion not to hunt. But, the job is one thing and your spiritual life is another. Tactical speaking, while on the job I wish more officers knew how to properly judge and assess others, it could save the lives of more officers. But, have you ever thought about using this same street skill, as a way to identify people that may need to accept and know Jesus Christ as their personal savior? In order to maximize your abilities as a Christian Cop, you need to be able to use the skills that God gave to you in a duel fashion. To protect yourself and others while at work, and to identify the spiritually hurting. This is where we have to pray and ask God to show us how not to always negatively judge and assess the people with whom we encounter. To help with this we should all remember the following Bible verse found in Matthew 7:1. *"Do not judge or you too will be judged. For in the same way you judge others, you will also be judged, and with the measure you use, it will be measured to you"*

Remember that sin can and does, entraps everyone. Your bosses who are not practicing Christians, may very well have a soft heart toward God, but the truth is, it may be covered up by a host of other things that Satan can use to blind us like fear, failure, addictions, success, power, and money just to name a few. In these cases, your answer is to pray. I once knew a Pastor whose wife would tell him whenever he would begin to display a *"human spirit,"* she would remind him that he needed to *"Go to God."* How often do we *"Go to God"* and ask for His help to get through our difficult work stresses. Probably not enough. Our bosses need our prayers and patience as well. Remember that in order to accomplish this difficult task of trying to understand our bosses from a Christian point of view, we need to ask God for the ability to look past all these distractions right to the heart. Because at the heart, everyone is hungry for God. Whether or not they will admit it, we were ALL created with that desire to know God.

The Shepherd and the Sheep

Throughout the Bible, God uses the illustration of the Shepherd and the sheep. Usually, this is used to identify the church and its flock of parishioners. But, I also believe that Christ uses the Shepherd illustration to talk about developing great leaders as well. This section is for those Christian leaders and supervisors who really want to make an outstanding Christ-like difference in their roles. For this exercise, I will need you to think about the job of a Shepherd and try to picture in your mind a Shepherd who is standing underneath a large oak tree holding his staff. Sitting on the ground next to him, is his assistant, the trusty sheep dog. Together, they work as a team, standing on a hillside watching over their flock as the sheep are grazing in the green meadows below them.

For me, whenever I think of this scene, I think of the Warner Brothers Looney Tunes cartoon character, *Sam the Sheepdog.* If you remember, Sam always looked like he was sleeping behind those long bangs hanging in front of his eyes. However, he was far from asleep and he was always on guard duty, watching everything. Nothing ever got past Sam. While this was a cartoon, in reality it isn't that far off from the truth.

There are two main purposes to the Shepherd and his sheep dog. One purpose is to keep watch over the flock to prevent the sheep from wandering away. The second is to prevent predators, like a wolf, from coming into the flock and stealing one of the sheep. One thing that you do not find is either the Shepherd, or his sheep dog running in the middle of the flock stirring up the sheep by demanding that they graze, and shouting at them to "stay here" or ordering them to "eat now." In other words, both the Shepherd and his trusty sidekick stay out of the business of the sheep and they do not "micro-manage" the sheep.

This is exactly what I believe God would desire of His Christian leaders, and what He would expect of them to lead others. They should remain at a distance watching over their responsibility without "barking" orders or demanding their subordinates to produce. Should one of their personnel were to go astray, then either the boss or his assistant should "correct" them back into the fold. Jesus also practiced this type of management technique with His disciples. The disciples were given the authority to heal and bless people in the name of God the father. However, there were times when the disciples did not have the faith or the ability to heal. In those times, Jesus was patience with them. He did not become easily angered. He did not "write up" the disciples or send them out to some obscure region to wander around aimlessly. Instead, Jesus saw the long range goal, the bigger plan which was to convert the world to become followers of God. And Jesus knew that He needed the disciples to do this work.

I am directing this to Christian supervisors now. You can never be the Godly leader that the Lord wants you to be if you cannot remain and watch your people from a distance as Jesus did with the disciples. This is called "Trust." Until, your staff gives you a reason not to trust them, as a Godly leader, you must trust them. Being a Godly leader requires great wisdom, strength, character, and endurance, but the Christian leader who has accepted Christ into their lives can always count on the presence of the Holy Spirit of God. This is what makes us different from other police supervisors.

Just as God allows His creation, which is man, to make mistakes, so too can we as supervisors can learn from the mistakes of others. Remember, it is your responsibility to teach and lead your subordinates as a way for them to learn from you. Being a great leader is not about *"You"* or whether or not you will get a raise, impress the Chief or Sheriff, or whether you can promote higher up the ranks so you can earn more money.

Instead, it is about how you teach your employees to be great leaders by showing them how to lead with trust and to make proper decisions on their own. There is great responsibility to being a law enforcement supervisor. As a leader, go the extra mile to make a difference in the lives of your subordinates.

Read the following Bible verse found in Job 31:13. I like what the Message Bible says about this verse; *"Have I ever been unfair to my employees when they brought a complaint to me? What, then, will I do when God confronts me? When God examines my books, what can I say?"*

Small Group Questions - Discuss your answers with your small group and write your answers below.

By giving us difficult bosses, what do you think God is trying to teach us?

1. _____

2. _____

3. _____

Leadership Skills from a Dictator?

Back in 1996, when I was promoted to the rank of Sergeant, it was suggested by the Sheriff that all newly promoted supervisors read two *"outstanding"* books on leadership and management. The first was *'Lincoln on Leadership'* and the second, was *'Mein Kampf'* by Adolph Hitler. I couldn't believe it, the Sheriff of our county at that time, (*1989-1999*) actually endorsed reading a book by the world's largest mass murderer and racist! We were to *"review"* this book for its management techniques and supposed leadership examples and not the content of the book. What I found was that our Sheriff and his staff were not only *"off their rocker"* but they were not alone in this thinking. During that time, there were a number of other law enforcement officials who had also endorsed this book to be used as a tool for newly promoted managers. Thank God that the Lord removed this Sheriff after his second term in office, and before I had a chance to read that book. Not that I ever would have. Instead, I began to promote two other Christian books on management techniques that I did share with my fellow Sergeants. The two books were *'The Management Methods of Jesus'* by Bob Briner, and *'The*

Small Group Chapter Thought - Always remember to let your inspiration for greatness as a leader come not from former mass murderers and dictators, but rather from divine inspiration such as from the Bible and from the teachings of Jesus Christ

---

Top Ten Mistakes Leaders Make' by Hans Finzel. Both of these books I would strongly endorse for any law enforcement supervisor. After reading these books, more than one of my fellow Sergeants told me that they had no idea that the Bible could speak so precisely about managing people. Additionally, every leader, or potential supervisor should use the illustration of the *"Shepherd and his Sheep dog"* to help them become an outstanding Godly supervisor.

A Changed Heart

Think of the times that you worked for, or may currently be working for, a difficult supervisor. List some things that Christ can do to change a supervisor's hardened heart.

1. _____

2. _____

3. _____

Pray every day for your leaders. Pray that they will make the right decisions. Pray that you can make a positive impact on them. Pray that the Lord will use you as His tool to develop and lead those under your charge to be great leaders like Joseph, Jacob, and Moses, and others in the Bible.

ANSWER KEY FOR BECOMING PEACEKEEPERS IN THE WORKPLACE

1. Peacekeepers take the **INITIATIVE** .

2. Peacekeepers **EMPATHIZE** with others.

3. Peacekeepers focus on the **ISSUE** not the person.

4. Peacekeepers are **FLEXIABLE** and willing to compromise

Chapter Thirteen

Enlarging Your Jurisdiction

"The mission for all Christian Cops"

Bible Verse - *"Jabez was more honorable than his brothers. His mother had named him Jabez, saying, "I gave birth to him in pain. Jabez cried out to the God of Israel, oh, that you would bless me and enlarge my territory! Let your hand be with me, and keep me from harm so that I will be free from pain. And God granted his request."* - 1 Chronicles 4:9-10

In law enforcement we are all bound by our jurisdictions. These limits may be your patrol zone, your assigned districts, the city limits, the county line or state line, or for federal law enforcement as far as judicial districts or the international waters. But too often, we in law enforcement protect these jurisdictions as if it they were our favorite "fishing holes." When this happens we are actually developing a protectionist attitude which sets us up for failure by allowing us not too cooperate with others agencies or sometimes even those within our own agency. This in turn, can make our agencies ineffective to the communities that we serve.

A few years back I was assigned to work as part of an FBI bank robbery task force for a string of bank robberies that were occurring in our community. During a task force meeting in which there were approximately one hundred FBI Special Agents along with about fifty state and local law officers in attendance we could hear a discussion growing louder from the back of the room until it reached a full blown shouting match. This shouting match then led to physical blows. The people involved were quickly ushered out of the room by a gang of other agents. We found out later that this altercation turned out to be two FBI Special agent supervisors who were from two different offices. Their argument begin when they couldn't agree over which FBI office had primary "jurisdiction" over the many bank robberies. These two agents lost sight of the main mission which was to catch the bank robbers and not what individual or office would get the credit.

Our Jurisdictions

While jurisdictional boundaries are a *"necessary evil"* for our roles as law enforcement officers, they are not acceptable for our roles as Christian officers. In order to make a difference in the lives of both our fellow officers, as well as the citizens that we are paid to *'protect and serve'*, we need to enlarge our spiritual jurisdictions. But what exactly does enlarging my *"spiritual jurisdiction"* mean? Simply put it means that if we are going to serve God, then we are going to have to step outside of our comfort zones. Just like we really can't solve crimes riding around with the windows rolled-up and the "juke jam" turned up, we also can't serve to lead others to Christ if we don't want to leave the comfort of our spiritual minds.

The Bible refers to jurisdiction as *"territory"*. Our study Bible verse from 1st Chronicles, commonly referred to as the *"Prayer of Jabez"* has been debated and interpreted by Biblical scholars for generations. Many of whom believe that this prayer is a selfish Biblical verse for increasing one's own material wealth. In fact, when you read this Bible verse for the first time and read the word 'territory', you probably thought of some property that you either own, or have some responsibility over. But increasing one's material wealth was not a priority of Jesus.

Small Group Scripture Reading - Read the *"Prayer of Jabez"* as found in 1 Chronicles 4:9-10 *"And Jabez was more honorable than his brethren: and his mother called his name Jabez, saying, because I bare him with sorrow. And Jabez called on the God of Israel, saying, Oh that thou wouldest bless me indeed, and enlarge my coast, and that thine hand might be with me, and that thou wouldest keep me from evil, that it may not grieve me! And God granted him that which he requested."*

Throughout the Bible, Jesus often spoke about giving larger responsibility based on what we as Christians do with the small responsibilities that we are given. For example of this is the parable of the talents (ten minas) as found in Luke 19:11-27 in this story Jesus said to them the following; *"Well done, my good servant!' his master replied. 'Because you have been trustworthy in a very small matter, take charge of ten cities. The second came and said, 'Sir, your mina has earned five more. His master answered, 'You take charge of five cities.'*

Small Group Scripture Reading - *"Whoever can be trusted with very little can also be trusted with much."* - Luke 16:10

Small Group Discussion Question - Share your answers with your small group.

"After reading the "Parable of the Talents," what do you think that Jesus is trying to tell us"?

Small Group Question – Answer and discuss among your group

1. *By praying to God, do you believe that Jabez had faith?*

2. *Do you believe that Jabez was stepping outside of his own comfort zone by asking for God's blessing?*

God Enlarges Our Territory for Him

Often times, the only reason God will enlarge a person's territory is when He knows that person will use it responsibly just as found in Luke 19:11-27. In other words, when God knows that an individual will be a steward over what is entrusted to them by God. However, many of us fail to understand that simple word, *"entrust"*. Throughout the Bible, God uses the word entrust to show faithfulness with the things that He gives us. God truly wants to increase our territory so that we can have a greater spiritual influence in the world around us. Personally, I can think of no other profession as that of a law enforcement officer, which can have such a direct and profound influence on the citizens of this world as that of a police officer. Can you?

Small Group Question - Can you name another profession in which one individual can have such a direct dominion and influence? If so, list your answers below.

*   _____

*   _____

*   _____

*   _____

Strategically Placed

Sometimes, we tend to forget that as law enforcement officers, God has strategically placed us in the best position possible in order to make an impact on the life of someone else. While it may not seem like it, enforcing the law and affecting the arrest of an individual can have a positive and lasting effect. Unfortunately, the arrested individual and their family members do not view law enforcement as an answer to their prayers. In fact they probably think the exact opposite.

Small Group Exercise - Answer each question by reading this statement first;

"By arresting someone, and enforcing the law you may have......

- Removed a person from society who was prepared to hurt or injured by someone else.

- *Finally forced (by court order) a person to receive some treatment for their problem such as in the cases of substance abuse, where treatment may have a lasting and positive effect or an individual, or on their family.*

- *Answered prayer. By having a positive impact on the victim of a particular crime by offering closure and peace of mind*

- *Turned a life over to Christ.*

What a responsibility! If you noticed, the above examples only center with the arrest of someone and does not take into account the simple and regular everyday contacts that law enforcement officers can have with people. How many crimes and potential crimes, may have been adverted simply by your presence, or by a word or deed that may have seemed harmless to you at the moment? As an officer you have the authority to make a difference in the life of someone each and every day that you go to work.

Small Group Discussion / Question *– "What will you do with the small responsibilities that you are given?"*

Small Group Question - Based on the above example can you recall any specific incidents in which you may have been someone's *"answered prayer"?* Share your response with the group.

- _____

- _____

Buddha Doesn't Like Egg McMuffin

I am always amazed at how many people believe that by simply tithing at Church, or by doing small tasks; they feel that they have performed some great act for God. They believe that God now owes them something in return for their service. They say things like "See, I'm a good person I give to my Church so why did that have to happen to me?" or they may believe, "Singing in the choir is my service to God and I really don't need to get involved in anything more". These people do not realize just how far off the mark from God they really are.

Once, on a Saturday morning my wife and I went furniture shopping. As we made our first stop at a local furniture store, we noticed a lady coming out the front door of the business carrying an Egg McMuffin on a paper plate with a side of hash browns. Sticking out from the middle of the Egg McMuffin was a lit incense stick. Now, this was a site to behold and she definitely had my attention. I was extremely curious as I watched her place this food on the sidewalk in front of the store. Bend down and chant a prayer. I mustered all the "political correctness" that I could and I asked her what she was doing? She explained that she was *"honoring Budda with an offering to bless her store for the day."* Well, we didn't buy anything that day and I can only image that no one else did either. Because about six weeks later when my wife and I went back out looking for additional furniture pieces we stopped at the same store but it was now closed and out of business. I can only assume that Budda didn't like his Egg McMuffin meal that day.

The lesson learned here is that we cannot treat God in the same manner as this store owner treated her Buddha. You see, God doesn't want our meaningless and trivial offerings, and that includes our money and our talents if it is not 'freely given' back to Him. So, you should remember that by praying the "Prayer of Jabez" it will not increase your monetary territory and is not intended to. However, pray that it will increase your spiritual territory for God's will to be done and not our own. That is the type of prayer that God wants to hear.

God Is Not a Genie in a Bible

It is important to remember that God is not some *"Genie in a Bible"*, waiting to be coaxed out so He can grant you three wishes. Rather, prayer is about aligning your heart and mind with God's purposes. With that said, by praying the "Prayer of Jabez" God can enlarge your jurisdiction for His purposes, provided that your heart is in the right place. Always remember that as a Christian law enforcement officer whose has already accepted Christ into your life, God has placed you in a position of authority for His purpose, and not your own. Remember, God didn't allow you to succeed over hundreds of other people for your position as a way to satisfy your own agenda but rather HIS agenda.

Faith is the Answer

Has your faith been tested? Do you feel that you can no longer have faith in God because of your questions, struggles, and disappointments? Too many officers have chosen to loose their faith in God because of something that has either happened to them or happened to someone they loved. Maybe, they lost a partner, a child, or a spouse and the only way to understand the tragedy is to blame God. But instead of blaming God when tragedies occur we need to turn to Him for our strength. Our tragedies should remind us that this world was never intended to be our final home. It is important to remember that our time on earth as we know it is only temporary as told to us in James 4:14

> **Small Group Scripture Reading -** As a group, take turns reading the following Bible verses;
>
> * *Hebrews 11:13-16*
>
> * *James 4:14*

Whenever we find ourselves in these difficult situations the important question to ask is not "Why God did this happen to me?" but instead, we should be asking "What is it that God is trying to teach me?" Jesus tells us in Mark 9:23 that we are to have faith by saying; *"Anything is possible, if you only believe"*.

Also, it is important to remember what we are told in the book of James 2:14-26 that *"So you see, it isn't enough just to have faith. Faith that doesn't show itself by good deeds is no faith at all--it is dead and useless. Now someone may argue, "Some people have faith; others have good deeds." I say, "I can't see your faith if you don't have good deeds, but I will show you my faith through my good deeds." Do you still think it's enough just to believe that there is one God? Well, even the demons believe this, and they tremble in terror! Fool! When will you ever learn that faith that does not result in good deeds is useless?*

What this verse tells us is that without having both faith and service working together for God, little can ever be accomplished. However, working with faith and deeds in God, great things can be accomplished! We in the profession of law enforcement should have a "proactive" faith in God.

Small Group Scripture Reading - Read these Bible verses among the small group members.

• *"For we are God's workmanship, created in Christ Jesus to do good works, which God prepared in advance for us to do."* - *Ephesians 2:10*

• *"He chose capable men from all Israel and made them leaders of the people, officials over thousands, hundreds, fifties and tens."* - *Exodus 18:25*

There are four ways that you can build on your faith.

- **Utilize my Imagination** - Read the following Bible verse from Ephesians 3:20 (NIV); *"Now to him who is able to do immeasurably more than all we ask or imagine, according to his power that is at work within us,"*

- **Neutralizing my Fears** – Read the following Bible verse from 2 Timothy 1:7 (NIV). *"For God did not give us a spirit of timidity, but a spirit of power, of love and of self discipline".*

- **Maximizing my Comfort Zone** – Read the Bible verse from Luke 19:26; "He replied, I tell you that to everyone who has, more will be given, but as for the one who has nothing, even what he has will be taken away."

- **Verbalizing my Expectations** – Read the Bible verse from Mark 11:23-24 (NIV) "I tell you the truth, if anyone says to this mountain, 'Go, throw yourself into the sea,' and does not doubt in his heart but believes that what he says will happen, it will be done for him. Therefore I tell you, whatever you ask for in prayer, believe that you have received it, and it will be yours."

Chapter Fourteen

Getting Connected With God

"When Cops Need a Back-Up"

Bible Verse - *"For where two or more come together in my name, there I will be also"- Matthew 18:20*

When you hear the word *"connected,"* what comes to mind? For me, I think of a light bulb being connected to an electrical outlet. When left alone, the bulb by itself does nothing. However, once you connect a light bulb to the electrical circuit, you produce light. Being connected to a small group or a church family is very similar. If you come to church, or participate in a small group study out of obligation to God, or to someone else then you are not connected to the body of Christ. You are simply like a light bulb that is not connected to any electrical current. If this sounds like you, then you need to check out your connection to see if you "plugged in" to God. If not, it is never too late to accept Christ into your life.

False Impressions

Many of us have the false impression that as long as I believe in God and don't violate any of the Ten Commandments then *"I'm alright in my life"* with God. Maybe you believe that you don't need to attend Church because you can quietly mediate to yourself and thereby still worship God. There are many people who believe that they can watch a Church service on television, or listen on the radio, and that is worshiping God.. They think, "I am good enough alone without anyone's help and God knows it." Well, that's where you are wrong and here's why. God never intended for worship to be an individual act. Read the following Bible verse as found in Romans 12:5 (NIV) *"so in Christ we who are many form one body, and each member belongs to all the others."* You see, trying to be a 'good Christian' all alone, without being connected to other believers is like going to a hot in progress call without a back-up unit it's neither smart nor gives you any advantage. Read the following Bible verse from *Ecclesiastes 4:12 "Though one may be overpowered, two can defend themselves. A cord of three strands is not quickly broken"*

We Each Need Spiritual Back-up

Like many of you, I grew up in the 1970's. During that time I watched a lot of police TV shows. In fact, it's probably the reason I become a cop. There was 'Dragnet'; 'Adam-12' (my favorite); 'Hawaii 5-0', and 'Starsky and Hutch', just to name a few. The one thing that all these TV shows and the officer characters had in common with one another was that they all had a partner. Starsky had Hutch, McGarrett had Dano, and Malloy had Reed.

While each one of these TV cops had a partner to help fight against the bad guys, so we as Christian cops need to have a spiritual partner as well. This is one of the reasons for participating in this study to help develop spiritual partners. In Romans 12:5, the Bible tells us that *"so in Christ we who are many form one body, and each member belongs to all the others."* To fellowship and be around other believers is not only necessary for success as a Christian, it is mandated by God as found in Hebrews 10: 24-25: *"And let us consider how we may spur one another on toward love and good deeds. Let us not give up meeting together, as some are in the habit of doing, but let us encourage one another–and all the more as you see the Day approaching."*

Being Connected

Law enforcement officers have always enjoyed the company of other cops. You know, the shift parties, the "choir practice" (which has nothing to do with signing in the church choir), or just hanging out with one another after work. However, this is not the type of "connection" that I am talking about. Connection is just another term for Commitment. It was always the intention of Jesus Christ that we be committed, or connected, to other Christian believers and to the "body of Christ" which is the Church.

God never intended for us to spiritually go it alone. It is extremely important for us to surround ourselves with other believers and show Christ's love through our Christian support of one another. When we attempt to worship God alone we are actually going against what the Bible commands us to do. The Bible in Romans 12:5 (NIV) states *"In Christ we who are many form one body, and each member belongs to all the others."* This is one of the main ideas behind the "PeaceKeepers" Bible study.

Contrary to our different personal idea of how to worship God, the fact remains that you cannot cloister yourself into your home, draw the drapes and still be worshipping God. Read Romans 14:19 (NLT) *"So then, let us aim for harmony in the church and try to build each other up.* Still, in the book of Galatians 6:2 we are told to; *"Share each other's troubles and problems. And in this way obey the law of Christ."* A favorite saying of mine is, *"We serve better when we are connected together."* What this saying tells us is that when we accept Christ into our hearts and follow His teachings as outlined in the Bible, and when we allow ourselves to be committed to the support of fellow Christian officers, and committed to the support of a loving Church family, your spiritual life can reap some tremendous benefits. Some of these benefits include the following;

- Leading an officer to become more spiritually stronger. By faith and studying God's word, that is the Bible.

- Finding that you will be a better cop while on the job with a much longer patience level.

- Having a stronger family life and being a better parent to your children, as well as a better spouse to the one that you love.

Prayerfully, you are reading this book as part of a small group study consisting of other Christian officers. If so, then you are already fulfilling one of God's commandments. If not, and you are reading this book as an individual, I would highly encourage you to find just one other officer to share this book with. It is my sincere prayer that God will lead you to reach out to other fellow officers by starting up your own connection group. Don't use this study as a way to cloister yourselves like some monk. Don't stuff this book up on some shelf to gather dust. Give it to someone else. Use your group, and this book as a tool to reach out to your fellow officers. Make a connection for God today!

Small Group Question – Take turns and answer the following questions as a group.

- *Do you feel that you are now "connected" to a body of other Christian believers?"*

- *Do you believe that you can be saved by God alone and without any other Christian support?*

- *When you worship or study God in the company of other believers how does it make you feel?*

A Christian Commitment

Being *"connected"* also means that we need to be committed to living a life with Jesus Christ as well as being committed to the body of Christ, which is the Church. Simply stated, you need to make time to attend a church service and be actively involved in practicing and following the teaching of Jesus Christ. So, the question really becomes "Why can't I worship God by myself without having to get "touchy feely with others"? Because, Church is where other believers are found in which God wants you to be connected with. He doesn't want you to be "connected" with fellow believers down at Joe's Pool Hall or the local Cop bar. When we are connected to a Church body of other believers you support and learn from one another through our weaknesses, problems, and our triumphs. It also provides us with a spiritually grounded Christian support network that will love you unconditionally.

I once heard a great analogy that describes being connected to a Church body. It is like a boat that is not properly tied up to a dock. A storm comes and tosses the boat out to sea where it drifts lifelessly. Because the boat was not properly docked and tied off to a land mass, it became lost in a giant sea. Being "connected" or "committed" to a group of other believers is the same way. It provides a spiritual safety rope for us to cling too. Additionally, membership in a Church is a public commitment to your life as a Christian. Just as when you accepted Christ into your life and are baptized, the act of baptism is a public expression of an inward belief that you want others to see.

But, what if I am not physically able to participate in church? If you are elderly, sick, or injured, and not able to participate in a church service, then God would certainly understand. However, if you are simply too busy with other projects on a weekend, or if you are so weighted down with monetary debt that you must work every Sunday, or, if you seem to be indifferent towards your fellow believers, then you will need to "go to God" to address your spiritual heart. Ask Him to help show you the way to get your Godly priorities in order and proper path to take.

As Christians who have accepted Christ into their life and who are active in the body of Christ (the Church) there are three main benefits that we receive when we are spiritually connected to other believers. First, there is the joy of fellowship and living in a spirit of Christian love with other believers. Second, there is the support of a spiritual network of other believers. And lastly because there is an opportunity to make a spiritual difference in the life of someone else. Our struggles and troubles can be a spiritual learning experience for those who may be new to a Church setting.

Also, we must never forget that Jesus himself was committed to the Church and that Jesus loved the Church so much that he referred to it as the *'Body of Christ'*. 1 Corinthians 12:27, *"Now you are the body of Christ, and each one of you is a part of it."* \

Small Group Scripture Reading - Read the following Bible verse from Hebrews 10:23-25:

"Without wavering, let us hold tightly to the hope we say we have, for God can be trusted to keep his promise. Think of ways to encourage one another to outbursts of love and good deeds. And let us not neglect our meeting together, as some people do, but encourage and warn each other, especially now that the day of his coming back again is drawing near".

Small Group Exercise - Write some examples of why it is important to be connected to a Church family? Discuss your answers with your group.

- _____

- _____

- _____

Why Being Connected is Important to God

Here are some reasons why it is important for Christians to participate and be involved in small groups, or as part of a Church family. Answer each of the following by first stating the sentence and the appropriate bible verse.

"By being connected to a Church family, or group it ....

•... Shows our love for God - *"You are worthy, O' Lord, to receive glory and honor and power."* - Rev. 4:11

• **... Brings a special visitation of the Lord's presence** -*"For where two or more are gathered together in my name, I am there also."* - Matt. 18:20

• **... provides fellowship with other Christians** - *"But if we are living in the light of God's presence, just as Christ is, then we have fellowship with each other, and the blood of Jesus, his Son, cleanses us from every sin."* - 1 John 1:7

• **... Provides accountability to spiritual leadership-***"Remember your leaders who first taught you the word of God. Think of all the good that has come from their lives, and trust the Lord as they do."* - Hebrews 13:7

•........strengthens prayer habits - *"I also tell you this: If two of you agree down here on earth concerning anything you ask, my Father in heaven will do it for you. For where two or three gather together because they are mine, I am there among them."* - Matthew-18:19-20

• **... Honors the Lord's Day** - *"Remember to observe the Sabbath day by keeping it holy. Six days a week are set apart for your daily duties and regular work, but the seventh day is a day of rest dedicated to the LORD your God. On that day no one in your household may do any kind of work"* - Exodus 20:8-10

Cops a Mixture of Emotions

Over the years, I have found that the majority of law enforcement officers who I have encountered to be an emotional mixture of personality types. The vast majority seem to follow this pattern. See if you recognize yourself in the following descriptions.

- *extremely private*

- *quite*

- *introverted*

- *at times moody*

- *prefer not to socialize with anyone outside of their close-knit circle of family or friends*

While these emotions are extremely understandable, they are not an excuse for how we treat others. As police officers, we deal with so much negativity directed towards us on a daily basis that it tends to draw us away from society. We began to think, "Why should I tell anyone what I do for a living?" The fear is that it could only draw you into some conversation about "the last time I got a speeding ticket," or "I called the cops five times for a neighborhood party and they didn't do anything about it" or, "Why do I see so many cops hanging around the donut shop?"

Small Group Discussion /Question - Discuss among your group the following questions. Be honest in your answers.

- Have you known any police officers who have been divorced, committed suicide, or have battled alcoholism as a result of a job in law enforcement?
- Do you know if they were connected to a Church family?
- If you knew these same officers today, looking back, what could you have done differently for them to help them escape their situation?

Small Group Exercise - Write below some examples of what you, personally could do to lead others to Christ.

- _____

- _____

- _____

- _____

- _____

Write the first names only of any officers that you know are in need of prayer. Ask your small group to pray this week for them

- _____

- _____

- _____

- _____

- _____

Chapter Fifteen

Combating Negativity
In the Workplace

"Maintaining a Christian Workplace"

Bible Verse- *"God is faithful. He will keep the temptation from becoming so strong that you can't stand up against it. When you are tempted. He will show you a way out so that you will not give in to it." - 1 Corinthians 10:13(b)*

All of us have done our share of complaining about our jobs at one time or another and let's face it, cops are great complainers myself included. We complain about our pay, we complain about our lack of equipment, we complain about our bosses, we complain about the politicians that have control over our budgets, we complain about our policies, the citizens, and our co-workers. Law enforcement seems to have more of their 'unfair share' of whiners than any other public safety position. This is not to say that many of our complaints are not justified but rather, we need to remember that when we dwell upon our disappointments, our discouragements, and the negativity that exists within our profession, it not only brings us stress, but it can also impact us negatively in our spiritual heart.

I can remember in the early days of my law enforcement career when I would come home from working a twelve hour shift so stressed out that it would take me hours of non-stop ranting and raving at my wife about my day's activity. I would keep going over it in my mind again and again until finally, my wife would say, "Why don't you just quit your job? You are so unhappy." Instead of turning my problems and issues over to God I was burdening my wife with them. As a partner to my spouse, I did not have the right to burden her with my work stress. Sure, I can discuss it with her and should. However, I do not possess the right to "emotionally vomit" on her, my children, my parents, the citizenry, or my co-workers. When we allow ourselves to "stress out" in front of others we are committing a sin. The Bible in the book of Philippians 4:6-7 states; *"Do not be anxious about anything, but in everything, by prayer and petition, with thanksgiving, present your requests to God. And the peace of God, which transcends all understanding, will guard your hearts and your minds in Christ Jesus."*

Any negativity allows us to sin, because it takes our minds away from God. Negativity does not allow us to trust God with our problems. Instead, we tend to handle them on our own by self-coping or relying on others to solve our problems for us instead of turning them over to God in prayer.

Some examples - All of us have been at times guilty of participating in workplace negativity. Let's take a look at some of these statements and see if you see yourself in any of these lines;

- "We didn't get our pay raises this year, but the brass sure got their pay increases."

- "How come I get transferred out of the unit, but the new rookie got to stay?"

- "If only the city (or county) government had given us the money we needed we would have had better equipment."

Once, I heard an officer tell a citizen that if they wanted a faster police response maybe they should call their elected officials and tell them to appropriate some more money for the department. While that may be a true and honest statement, in effect, that verbalization was an officer's internal stress being unleashed upon the citizenry. However, as Christians Ambassadors, we need to remember that we are to be a positive Christian example within our workplaces, as well as in our personal lives. We should not lead others astray by participating in, or contributing to our co-workers, disappointments, discouragement, and negativity within their jobs.. Once we do that everything else will fall into proper place. No one said that being a police officer was easy, and being a Christian Cop doesn't come any easier.

So Why All the Complaining?

So, have you ever wondered why law enforcement has so many of these complainers? Are you one of these whiners? Do you find yourself screaming like George Jetson running on the treadmill of life saying *"Help! Get me off this crazy thing."* First, in order to combat negativity in your workplace, you need to understand where it comes from.

Our disappointments, discouragements, and negativity within the workplace are not of God, but rather tools that Satan uses to throw Christians off the track of righteousness. We are told in James 1:13 not to blame God when we are tempted, because *"he doesn't use evil to tempt others"*. When we find ourselves becoming negative we are being tempted by Satan. We need to remember whenever this occurs, that God is not the enemy. God does not surround us with "negative nannies" in the form of co-workers always complaining as a way to bless and honor us. Instead, these are issues of personal pain that God wants to take on for us. The Bible in the book of Psalms 55:22 says, *"Give your burdens to the LORD, and he will take care of you. He will not permit the godly to slip and fall."* We need to learn to turn our problems over to God in prayer and worship.

Aren't We the Masters of Our Own Domain?

As humans, we do what humans do best, that is to think. And we start believing that we are the "masters of our own domains." We believe that we can handle most anything that comes our way. This way of thinking is exactly what the devil wants us to believe. That we don't need God to solve our problems, that we are smart enough to handle it on our own without any help from God. We must understand that Satan does not want God in our lives at all. So, we have to work extra hard at not being tempted and setting our minds to be more like Christ. We need to focus on Him and all that He has provided to us.

We are told in the book of James 1:12-13 that *"blessed is the man who perseveres under trail, because when he has stood the test, he will receive the crown of life that God has promised to those who love."*

Small Group Question – Discuss your answers openly with your small group members.

What are some of the ways that we can remain focused on God and less on our own way of negative thinking?

A Painful, Personal Experience in Negativity

One of my most shocking experiences at seeing negativity within the workplace occurred when I was promoted to the rank of Sergeant. I had only been promoted a few weeks and was in my first assignment as the new supervisor of a staff of twenty court security

Deputy Sheriffs when my Captain came to pay me a visit. But what he said shocked me. He didn't say, "Call me if you need anything," or ask me what he could do to help me. Instead, he said "you will soon find out that these guys are a bunch of whiners." As I stood there, dumbfounded, wondering how a cop could talk about others cops like that, he floored me with the next statement, which I have never forgotten. He said, "Yeah, they whine so much, that if I gave them a hundred dollars they would complain about the denomination." As much as I hate to admit it, I soon discovered that he was right. It wasn't long before I found that my office door became like one of those glass revolving department store doors followed by one complaining Deputy after the next.

I soon began to see that poor upper management had led to poor morale throughout our agency, and for some unknown reason these deputies that I once worked with now saw me as the person who could solve all of their problems. At the age of thirty-two, I was not prepared for the stress that followed. I soon realized that even though I had grown up believing in God and was a casual church attendee, in all this turmoil not once did I turn to God for help. Looking back, the reason that I did not turn to God was because I did not possess a strong enough Christian foundation and belief system in God that was necessary to understand what was happening in my career. I simply wasn't smart enough to realize that I was being tempted by evil.

It was hard for me to get past the idea that all this stress and turmoil wasn't about me. Besides, I thought that I could figure it out on my own. That this was some type of Sheriff's Department test of my skills to be a supervisor. But what I found out was that it wasn't about what management tools I possessed or didn't possess, and it wasn't about me personally. However, it was about me trying to tackle problems on my own without understanding how God can work daily in the lives of His people that choose to accept Him into their heart.

During this same time, our agency was going through much public controversy. There was so much negative talk and rumors being spread within the agency that the departmental managers put out a policy about negative talk and rumors. For me, it was the straw that broke the camel's back. I saw what disinterested and poor leadership had done to our department and after three years as a Sergeant, and fourteen years as a Deputy Sheriff I became one of many who threw up their hands and left the agency disgusted, stressed, and disillusioned. But I found out that by giving in, I wasn't hurting anyone except myself, In short, I played into Satan's game. To divide and conquer.

A Positive Change

But my experience was not a total loss. Little did I know that God was always there and wasn't about to give up on me. Leaving the Sheriff's Department caused me to have a desire to learn more about the different styles of management and leadership roles that existed in law enforcement. I wanted to know what style of leadership could cause such dissension within our ranks. I went back to college to study organizational management. Ultimately, this led me to obtain my undergraduate degree in management. But what I discovered, later, rather than sooner, was that none of this educational searching was necessary. There was no need to bury my head into books to find out what I was missing was a personal relationship with Jesus Christ. Even though I grew up believing that Christ was a part of my everyday life, in reality, I had shoved Him to the back of the closet, and allowed my law enforcement career to dictate my life. I can't help but wonder how many fellow cops, like myself, have treated God in this same way?

A New Start

Since that time, and with God's help, I have started a second law enforcement career with the federal government and God has given me yet another chance to once again become a first-line supervisor. But this time, instead of throwing up my hands and walking away from a career. God has given me the opportunity to try it again and, "prayfully," this time, I'll get it right. Now, I know how to lead with Christ. I put all my decisions, and those that I have been put in charge of, before God. I would be lying if I didn't tell you that there have been difficult times. It hasn't all been a "Christian cake-walk". I know that Satan will try to tempt me daily, to lead me off the path of righteous. However, leading with Christ as my boss makes the job a lot more bearable. I only wish I had learned this style of "management by Christ" years earlier.

Working without God

By the very nature of the position of a law enforcement officer, we are constantly dealing with the evil that exist in our society. Being exposed to such evil can cause us to lose our focus on God and start believing that we can handle any problem on our own. However, whenever we try to go it alone and attempt to handle things without calling on God it always tends to become "messed up". Instead, we should frequently turn to God and look for direction and guidance from Him through His word, the Bible. Often times, this will require us to set a Godly example for others and that can be scary. However, once we learn to trust and turn all of our problems and stressors over to the Lord is when we will experience a peace and a joy in our spiritual life that will carry over to our jobs as well as our home life.

Small Group Questions - Answer the following questions. Discuss your answers among your small group.

- Do you think that complaining and negativity can be tools of evil or just an expression of our human side?
- Do you believe that prayer can help us deal with our disappointments, and negative thoughts?
- Which one of the above Bible verses do you believe will personally help you in your struggle to combat negativity the workplace?

Small Group Exercise - Take turns reading the following Bible verses and see how they relate to us today in our workplaces. Select your favorite and explain to your group why you selected the verse.

Matthew 26:41 - *"Watch and pray so that you will not fall into temptation. The spirit is willing, but the body is weak."*

Luke 26:46 - "Why are you sleeping?" he asked them. "Get up and pray so that you will not fall into temptation."

2 Corinthians 3:18 - "As the spirit of the Lord works within us. We become more and more like him and reflect his glory   even more."

1 Corinthians 10:13(b) - *"God is faithful. He will keep the temptation from becoming so strong that you can't stand up against it. When you are tempted. He will show you a way   out so that you will not give in to it."*

Galatians 5:22 - *"But the fruit of the Spirit is love, joy, peace, patience, kindness, goodness, faithfulness."*

Proverbs 3: 5-6 - *"Trust in the Lord with all your heart and lean not on your own understanding. In all ways acknowledge   Him, and He will direct your paths."*

Small Group Exercise - Write in the first column, some negative thought or a complaint that you have either said or may have participated in. For example; foul talk with the guys. In the second column take clues from our Bible verses as listed on the previous page. Match up the appropriate positive response to the negative action.

NEGATIVE	POSITIVE

Some Tip Ideas to help remained focused on Christ while at work

- Have an accountability partner. Find a Christian co-worker who will allow you to pray with them during difficult times.

- Telephone your Christian friend or Chaplain whenever you may need spiritual help.

- If possible, play Christian music while at work. Either in your car, or while at your desk.

- Fellowship with other Christian law enforcement officers.

- Pray faithfully and specifically, for patience, and deliverance from temptations.

- Recognize that negativity is not of God, but rather of Satan and choose not to participate. Such as foul language.

- Make today the day that you change your behavior. Close the door on your old ways and start new and refreshed today.

- Pray the Serenity Prayer - *"God grant me the serenity to accept the things that I cannot change; the courage to change the things that I can; and the wisdom to know the difference". - Amen*

Chapter Sixteen

The Peer-Pressure We Experience

Bible Verse- *"Then Jesus was led by the Spirit into the desert to be tempted by the devil". - Matthew 4:1*

As adults, when we first think about the word "peer-pressure," we immediately think about young people succumbing to drugs or being pursued to purchase the latest "must-have" item that is being promoted by the media. But how many of us as police officers think about succumbing to pressures from our fellow adult peers? Chances are that as adults, we don't believe that peer-pressure can be an issue for us. In fact, many adults, and especially those within the law enforcement profession, feel that we are strong enough to not allow someone else to direct our motives. But the Bible refers to "peer pressure" as temptation. Temptation is a word that we all can relate to.

Let's take a look at the following definitions; According to the Merriam-Webster dictionary the word "peer" is defined as the following; "one that is of equal standing with another: equal; especially: one belonging to the same societal group especially based on age, grade, or status" The word "Temptation" is defined as the following; "The act of tempting or the state of being tempted especially to evil; enticement: something tempting a cause or occasion of enticement."

I believe that all of us can agree with that definition as being an accurate description for those of us in law enforcement. As police officers, we belong to the same societal group, which is law enforcement, and many of us are considered to have a common ground with others within our same profession. This is our equal standing.

Jesus Was Tempted by Satan

In Matthew chapter 4, we see that even Jesus was tempted by Satan. As a group read the following Bible verses. Matthew 4, verses 1-11. *"Then Jesus was led by the Spirit into the desert to be tempted by the devil. After fasting forty days and forty nights, he was hungry. The tempter came to him and said, "If you are the Son of God, tell these stones to become bread." Jesus answered, "It is written: "Man does not live on bread alone, but on every word that comes from the mouth of God. Then the devil took him to the holy city and had him stand on the highest point of the temple. If you are the Son of God," he said, "throw yourself down. For it is written: He will command his angels concerning you, and they will lift you up in their hands, so that you will not strike your foot against a stone." Jesus answered him, "It is also written: "Do not put the Lord your God to the test" Again, the devil took him to a very high mountain and showed him all the kingdoms of the world and their splendor. "All this I will give you," he said, "if you will bow down and worship me." Jesus said to him, "Away from me, Satan! For it is written: Worship the Lord your God, and serve him only. Then the devil left him, and angels came and attended him."*

Small Group Scripture Reading - Read the following Bible verse and answer the following questions;

1 Corinthians 10:13 - *"No temptation has seized you except what is common to man. And God is faithful; he will not let you be tempted beyond what you can bear. But when you are tempted, he will also provide a way out so that you can stand up under it."*

Questions / Discussions – Discuss the following questions as a group.

- What do you think the Bible is referring to when it says "what is common to man?"
- Is the words *"stand up under it"* the same as having *"faith"*?

Small Group Discussion - Answer the following questions as a group.

- What are some ways that you can be tempted while on the job? Discuss your answers openly with your group.

- Since we can all be tempted, what are some ways to combat temptation or peer-pressure? Write your answers below;

- _____

- _____

- _____

- _____

After reading 1 Corinthians 10:13 what do you think God means when he says *"he will not let you be tempted beyond what you can bear"*?

Negative and Positive Pressures

Peer pressure can be defined as being both a positive and a negative. For example, there is positive peer-pressure, such as attending a PeaceKeepers Bible study. The reason that you attend is because you want to be around fellow Christian law enforcement officers, and you want to learn more about the Bible and God. Negative peer-pressure is when you are tempted to do things that you otherwise would not normally do. In other words, things that can make you feel *"guilty"*, or things that you do out of guilt or pressure that someone else has placed over you. For example like going out with the guys after work instead of going home to your wife and kids. If we were to have any type of peer pressures we would want them to be positive. Remember that in all things we do, we should do them not for man, but rather for the glory of God. Remember to try and always turn a negative pressure into a positive pressure.

False Securities

You may falsely believe that as Christians, we have it easier than most non-Christians. In reality, as Christians we walk around with a big target for Satan on our foreheads. But Satan will do anything to get a Christian to turn to drugs, alcohol, pornography, and so on. If you give in to the devil, he will break your fellowship with God so the Lord can't use you, and evil will have succeeded. As a practicing Christian, and as one who has accepted Christ into your heart, you always have the strongest person on your side and God is always there! He tells us in the book of Hebrews 13:5; " I will never leave you, or forsake you". When you take a stand for what's right you are taking a stand for God. In this sense, Christians do have it easier. Because as stated in the above Bible verse from Hebrews, God promises never to abandon us or leave us.

How Does Temptation Work?

There are a number of different ways in which we can be tempted. The book of James 1 talks much about temptation and gives us a guide to go by. We are told in James 1:13-15 that *"each one is tempted when by his own evil desires, he is dragged away and enticed. Then, after desire has conceived, it gives birth to sin; and sin, when it is full-grown, gives birth to death" (NIV)*

For starters, temptation always begins with our own desires and temptation can trap us through the form of deception. We learn this in the book of James 1:14 when we are told the following; *"but each one is tempted when, by his own evil desire, he is dragged away and enticed."* The Bible gives us some great examples of people who were able to resisted temptation. Let's take a look at the people in the Bible who were tempted. Some yielded and some didn't. Here are just some of the highlights.

- Eve was tempted in the garden of Eden and she yielded and she led her husband into sin

- Noah was tempted to drink too much wine and he yielded and got drunk.

- Abraham was tempted to lie about his wife and he yielded and told a lie.

- Joseph was tempted to fornicate. But he did not allow temptation to get hold of him, and got out while the getting was good.

- Moses was tempted to take matters into his own hand and he yielded to the temptation and committed murder.

- David was tempted to lust and commit adultery and he yielded and brought great sin and shame to his kingdom.

- The Three Hebrew boys were tempted to worship a false god and they did not yield. As a result, they were thrown into a fiery furnace.

- Daniel was tempted to give up his prayer life and he did not yield and was placed in a den of lions and lived to tell about it.

- Peter was tempted to deny the Lord and he yielded but later repented and became one of the greatest preachers of the Jerusalem church.

- Thomas was tempted to doubt the Lord

In the Bible, James 4:7: says to submit yourself to God, for *"if you resist the devil he will flee from you."* Keep in mind that even Jesus Christ was tempted. The point being here is that there will never be a time when temptation cannot confront us. It is something we do not outgrow. It is common because we all face it. If Jesus can be tempted, what is to stop us, as mere humans, from being tempted by evil? Nothing.

Small Group Exercise - Look up as a group the following Bible verses and see if you can identify how Jesus was tempted. Discuss your answers with your group.

- by Satan (Matthew 4:1–10)

- by the Jewish leaders (Matthew 16:1)

- by Peter, His faithful disciple (Matthew 16:23)

Resisting Temptations

Jesus made several comments about resisting temptation. Remember what Jesus said at the Last Supper (Matthew 26:41). He said *"the spirit is willing but the flesh is weak, so we are to watch and pray that we will not fall into temptation"*. Part of the Lord's Prayer (Matthew 6:13) says, *"Lead us not into temptation, but deliver us from evil."* In 2 Peter 2:9 we read that the Lord knows how to rescue the godly from temptation. And in 1st Corinthians 10:13 tells us that God is faithful and that he will not allow temptation beyond what we can resist.

None of us are perfect and God knows that. God does not expect perfection from us, but He does expect us to do the best that we can. All of us have and all of us will continue to fall into temptation and sin from time to time because as Christians, we are under the constant watch of evil. However, with God's help He will deliver us from the temptation and the negative peer pressure that we face. We need to pray and turn to God for our strength and not try to fight against the demons of sin on our own.

Michael Dye

FINAL THOUGHTS

By having participated in this study, it is my sincere prayer that you have acquired the strength needed in order to make a spiritual difference in the lives of those who you encounter while in your job as a Christian law enforcement officer. If you have never accepted Christ into your heart then I pray that this Bible study will lead you to accept Jesus Christ, and become not only a follower but a "doer" of Christ word. It is also my hope that you can now began to see that you have both a Godly purpose and plan to your job. That no matter, how difficult the job of a law enforcement officer can become, you have the resources, and the spiritual strength to fight the demons that want to see a lawless society flourish. Through this study I hope that you now possess the strength to understand that the source of your personal stress and struggles in your job and in your home life is not something that God has given you and that there is no need to blame God for the troubles you have experienced in your lifetime

Finally, it is important to never forget that God wants us to positively influence the people whom we encounter while on duty. Always remember, that there is no one in a better position than you to make a difference for God in the life of a fellow citizen. Be a positive witness for Christ today. Go out and advance His kingdom through your job. God promises that He will never abandon us, leave us, or let us fail. No matter what anyone else thinks! May God bless you, and watch over you, as you serve as one of His PeaceKeepers!

Michael Dye is available for speaking engagements and personal appearances. For more information contact the publisher at:

ADVANTAGE BOOKS™
PO Box 160847
Altamonte Springs, FL 32716

To order additional copies of this book or to see a complete list of all **ADVANTAGE BOOKS™** visit our online bookstore at:

www.advantagebookstore.com

or call our toll free order number at: 1-888-383-3110

Longwood, Florida, USA

"we bring dreams to life"™
www.advbooks.com

About the Author

Michael Dye has spent over twenty years in the field of law enforcement working with both local and federal law enforcement agencies. He is a retired Deputy Sheriff with the rank of Sergeant, having spent over fourteen years with Volusia County Sheriff's Department in Daytona Beach Florida. Currently, Michael is employed as a federal law enforcement officer and based in Los Angeles, California. He is a graduate of Oklahoma City University with a Bachelors degree in Management and holds an Associate of Science degree in Criminal Justice.

Michael has served as a guest speaker for the United States Department of Justice-Office of Victimization, and for the State of Florida Attorney Generals Office in the area of elder abuse and neglect. He has been a frequent guest speaker at a number of Florida universities and high schools on how to conduct suspect interviews and teaching student's the techniques of peer counseling.

In 1995 he was the honored as a recipient of the American Legion Law Enforcement Officer of the Year Award and was a nominee in 1992 for President George H. Bush's Points of Light Campaign for his work with law enforcement volunteers.

Michael is a graduate of the Federal Law Enforcement Training Center in Glynco, Georgia *(2001)* and the State of Florida Basic Law Enforcement Training Academy *(1985)*.

Currently, he resides in Southern California with his wife, Jennifer, daughter Emily, and their three dogs. In his spare time, he enjoys traveling, writing, leading small groups at his Church, and spending time with the family.

Both Michael and his family are active members of Valencia Hills Community Church located in Valencia, California.

Printed in the United States
40439LVS00006B/1-51

9 781597 550314